P9-CFC-675

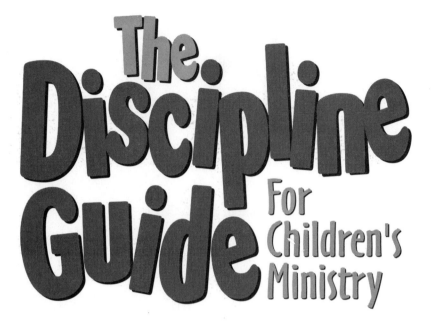

The Discipline Guide For Children's Ministry

by Jody Capehart and
Gordon and Becki West

Loveland, Colorado

This book is dedicated to the children at Prestonwood who make the discipling process a joy. A special note of thanks to Lois Keffer, who made this project a joyful experience.
Jody Capehart

This book is dedicated to Ashley and Emily, our own learning lab for discipline, and to all the children with whom we grew up as we learned to minister to kids. To Roy, Chip, Thom, and the other leaders of Central Christian Church who have served as godly models of spiritual leadership and have challenged us to continue growing and ministering to kids.
Gordon and Becki West

The Discipline Guide for Children's Ministry

Copyright © 1997 Jody Capehart, Gordon West, and Becki West

Chapters 1, 2, 4, and 7 written by Gordon and Becki West. Chapters 3, 4, 5, and 6 written by Jody Capehart.

Credits
Editor: Lois Keffer
Creative Development Editor: Paul Woods
Chief Creative Officer: Joani Schultz
Copy Editor: Julie Meiklejohn
Art Director: Jean Bruns
Assistant Art Director: Kari K. Monson
Cover Art Director: Lisa Chandler
Cover Illustrator: Steve Pica
Illustrators: Kate Flanagan, Randy Glasbergen, and Ron Wheeler
Production Manager: Peggy Naylor

Unless otherwise noted, Scriptures quoted from The Youth Bible, New Century Version, copyright © 1991 by Word Publishing, Dallas, Texas 75039. Used by permission.

All cartoons from *Clip-Art Cartoons for Churches,* Group Publishing, Inc. Used by permission.

Library of Congress Cataloging-in-Publication Data
Capehart, Jody.
    The discipline guide for children's ministry / by Jody Capehart and Gordon and Becki West.
       p.   cm.
    Includes bibliographical references.
    ISBN 1-55945-686-8
    1. Christian education of children. 2. Discipline of children–Religious aspects–Christianity. 3. Classroom management.
I. West, Gordon, 1959- . II. West, Becki, 1955- . III. Title.
BV1475.2.C319 1997
268'.432–dc21
                                     97-25331
                                        CIP

10 9 8 7 6 5 4 3 2 1   06 05 04 03 02 01 00 99 98 97
Printed in the United States of America.

Contents

93357

Introduction

Classroom discipline. The very words can trigger clammy palms and elevated heart rates in both teachers and kids. But it doesn't need to be that way. No teacher wants to be a drill sergeant. No child wants to be in trouble all the time.

What do teachers want? Classrooms full of kids who are excited to be in church, busily engaged in meaningful learning, and motivated to stay on task.

What do kids want? Exactly the same thing.

Think we're dreaming? The defense calls Christopher and Angela to the stand.

"I don't like when teachers let the class get out of control," says Christopher. "Sometimes teachers let it go crazy and then yell at the kids like it's their fault. Like one day the class was acting up a lot. The teacher couldn't get them to get quiet. So he got very angry and started to yell. He punished the whole class even though it was only a few who were acting up. Kids don't like that. It's not fair. I mean, like, what's the motivation for being good in the first place if you get punished with all the 'bad' kids?

"This is the kind of teacher I like. One day the class was acting up a lot. The teacher spoke in a kind, gentle voice and didn't yell. She asked them to 'Please settle down.' Even though her voice was gentle, we knew she meant business and we did settle down. The class got quiet and behaved well. She treated us with respect.

"I remember one time when I was little and a kid named Jason kept pushing me around. The principal went up to Jason, got on her knees, and looked right into his face. She took his hands and said: 'We use our hands to show love and to help. We do not hit.' He was better for about two days, and then he started hitting again. The principal went to him and made him tell her the rule and go to time-out. He threw a fit. I remember the principal saying, 'You may sit by me until you can remember the rules in our classroom.' He had to sit by her for several days. But I remember, she would just look at him or touch his shoulder when he was getting ready to hit. She never said a word. After a few days, he just quit hitting."

Now let's listen as Angela tells about her favorite teacher. "My teacher is one of the greatest people you could ever meet. She has the sweetest, most encouraging spirit most of the time. She knows when things are getting out of hand with children. To me, she handles them better than anyone I know. She doesn't raise her voice. She uses a gentle, firm voice and gives everyone a fair chance. That's what kids like in teachers—when they don't have favorites and discipline some kids and not others. My teacher is fair to all the kids."

If you're sighing and thinking, "Wow—I wonder if I could ever be the kind of teacher that kids would talk about that way," the answer is a resounding "Yes!"

Teachers who are masters at classroom discipline aren't born that way—they're trained. These teachers have learned what makes kids tick, how to teach kids of all learning styles, and the importance of respecting their students. Excellent teachers know and understand their students' needs and then create a classroom environment where every child's needs can be met.

This book offers you the tools you need to become that kind of teacher. You'll learn to honor children as Jesus honored them, to understand and meet their needs, and to recognize and deal with differences in personalities and learning styles. You'll find practical help for the nitty-gritty situations that come up in classrooms week in and week out. You'll receive expert advice on important issues such as how to deal with children with Attention Deficit Disorder (A.D.D.), how to work with parents, and how to improve your relationships with students. The final chapter offers training materials that will help you acquaint teachers with the principles of positive discipline as you work together to develop a unified discipline plan for your church.

Imagine being able to take all the energy that you've spent on crowd control and pour it into teaching kids to know, love, and follow Jesus. You can. Here's what you need to get started.

1 Kids in God's Kingdom

*God disciplines us to help us, so we can become holy
as he is (Hebrews 12:10b, New International Version).*

The names have been changed to protect the guilty—namely, all of us! The scene was a Wednesday night outreach meeting for fifth- and sixth-graders. The characters—and we use this word purposely—were two sixth-grade boys. This particular Wednesday they showed up with smiles on their faces because they thought that the leader of the Wednesday night children's program was out of town. Unbeknownst to the boys, he had returned. The first person they ran into was the leader's wife. Their question of her: "Is 'he' here? We always get in trouble when he's here."

This pair of sixth-grade boys had been attending the Wednesday night program for several weeks, behaving like typical kids. They talked when they were asked to be quiet, they were quiet when they were supposed to talk, they sat down when they were told to stand up, and they lay down when they were told to sit! The teaching staff was beginning to see them as problem children, and the boys were getting a negative view of church and of the children's leader himself.

Sound familiar?

What's wrong with this picture? Our goal had been to make kids feel welcome and loved. But something had backfired. We had inadvertently defeated our own purpose. If you've taken the time to pick up this book, it's probably because you've had a similar experience.

Does discipline have to be a negative thing? Is there a way to work with kids without constantly being "bugged" by their behavior? Can both the teacher and the student feel good about the discipline process?

Perhaps you've thought, "If only we could master this discipline thing, we could go on to the fun part of working with kids!" Unfortunately, even if we were to somehow "master" the techniques, children are always changing; we must continue to discipline them as they grow and take on new challenges.

Discipline problems are the number one reason volunteer teachers in the church cite as their reason for quitting. Children's workers need to learn sound principles and effective techniques of discipline just to survive!

It's time we stood back to take a careful look at what Scripture teaches us about the "whys" and "hows" of discipline.

Good Discipline Equals Discipling

The root word for discipline is disciple. So why is it that in the church we think of "discipling" as positive and "disciplining" as negative? Perhaps the problem with discipline in our classrooms begins with what we believe about discipline.

Thorndike/Barnhart's Advanced Dictionary defines discipline as "training, especially training of the mind or character; a trained condition of order and obedience." This obedience doesn't refer to mindlessly jumping at someone's command. Good discipline, like discipling, trains kids to develop self-control. Training is the key word here—not punishment.

When we disciple children, we correct them in a way that shows them they are loved. When kids sense our loving concern, they're much more willing to emulate our values and our relationship with God. Good discipline is guidance toward right behavior, which is much more effective than punishment for wrong behavior.

> The key to discipling children is to model Christlike behavior for them while assuring them in every way possible that we truly love them.

Discipline forms the very core of our Christian education programs. We don't teach kids so that they'll be able to regurgitate facts from the Bible or so they'll do whatever we say whenever we say it. We teach to change lives!

The goal of discipline in our Christian classrooms must be to train children to be Christlike. We want kids to internalize the biblical principles we teach and to grow in their personal relationships with God. Discipline is an ongoing process in which teacher control gradually gives way to Christian self-control or, should we say, *God-control.*

God's Word acknowledges the painful part of the discipline process:

> *No discipline seems pleasant at the time, but painful. Later on, however, it produces a harvest of righteousness and peace for those who have been trained by it (Hebrews 12:11, NIV).*

Let's face it—a child does not say, "Thank you for this discipline because I know that it will produce a harvest of righteousness and peace." Children see discipline as synonymous with punishment. We need to carefully and continually demonstrate to kids that our goal is not to shame and blame; rather, our goal is to help them become like Christ.

The Teacher as Mentor

When we see discipline as a spiritual mentoring process, it takes on even greater significance. As mature Christians, we are passing on to younger, less mature people practical ways to live like Jesus.

Although it's a bit scary to admit, the far greater share of responsibility for this process lies with the teacher. The teacher controls almost everything about the condition of the classroom (outside of the physical structure itself), including the atmosphere and mood, the comfort level, the preparedness or lack of it, and the style of discipline. The teacher's beliefs about children and his or her approach to classroom management will greatly impact students' behavior.

What's the best approach to discipline in the classroom? It's more simple than you might imagine: we must require ourselves to understand the needs of kids and prepare ourselves to meet those needs appropriately. When we apply ourselves to accomplishing these ends, we'll stop most behavior problems before they get started! Above all, we need to always bear in mind that our students are children of God who deserve to be treated with respect and dignity.

Why Do Children Misbehave, Anyway?

Most kids want to please adults—they have no overarching goal to get in trouble and stay there! They misbehave for a reason. Let's consider some of the reasons:

● **Ignorance of the rules.** Never assume that kids know what's expected of them. Rules need to be spelled out regularly in class, and the consequences need to be stated clearly and applied consistently. Begin each new class with a discussion of your expectations, and review them every month or as you see your class starting to forget them. Review expectations again after a long break or special event.

Kids will quickly discover which rules you are serious about. Research has shown that kindergartners take no more than one week to discover which rules are real and which are "empty." Empty rules are those you only verbalize and never enforce. It's best to keep your rules to a minimum and expect the children to follow all of them.

● **Conflicting rules.** Our students come from a variety of home situations. Each family undoubtedly has a different set of expectations, as does each teacher. With most elementary-age children, one or more school teachers also contribute expectations. Kids can get confused! It boils down to this: What's OK in one setting may be unacceptable in another.

At home, some kids have to compete with one or more siblings to get the things they want. When those kids carry their competitive behavior into the Sunday school room, they may drive you up a wall!

At school, a first-grader may be allowed to sit on his or her desk-top. If this is against the rules at church, you may find the student innocently disobeying.

In some cases, a church may offer Sunday school followed by a children's worship time. Suppose the first teacher allows kids to talk freely, but the second requires kids to raise their hands before speaking. How confusing to a child—especially if both sessions are held in the same classroom. (See Chapter 7 for tips on setting and agreeing upon discipline standards for your church.)

As a teacher, your family life may be very different from that of your students. Your understanding of appropriate behavior and good manners may conflict with the expectations of a child's parent or other caregiver. We need to be aware of these differences and not fault kids because we assume that other authorities in their lives set the same standards we do.

● **Frustration.** When children are frustrated, they misbehave. The typical response to a sense of failure or frustration is aggression.

Sometimes the teacher can be a source of frustration. All of us need to take an honest look at things we do that might increase our kids' frustration levels. Some teachers call on the same kids over and over rather than encouraging answers from everyone. When a teacher is irritated with a child, that teacher may expect misbehavior. This kind of negative attention almost always becomes a self-fulfilling prophecy. A teacher's sour mood will inevitably affect his or her students.

Frustration can also come from other students. Kids who are not well-liked and who are less socially adept may get picked on or ignored. The resulting pain often leads to aggressive or disruptive behavior. Children will not behave well when they don't feel good about themselves or about being in your class.

If a project is too difficult or not age-appropriate, you'll see frustration mount. Children will often react in negative ways if they constantly feel rushed and unable to complete the activities you select. A sense of accomplishment and an assurance of reasonable success is a must for children to be at their best.

● **Boredom.** Think of boredom as the opposite end of the spectrum from frustration. Whereas difficult activities can frustrate children, a lack of meaningful activities will bore them.

The needed ingredient here is relevance. For learning to take place, kids need to see how classroom activities relate to their interests, their needs, and their lives outside the church or classroom. Irrelevance breeds boredom, and boredom quickly breeds disruptive behavior.

Can we make every activity entirely relevant and age-appropriate so that all our students will be motivated all the time? Not likely. But we can be prepared to provide choices. If one activity bombs, we can let students move on quickly to something else. Giving kids a choice between two activities makes both activities more desirable!

● **Displaced anger.** When everything else seems in order in your classroom but a child acts out or becomes overly emotional, you may be dealing with displaced aggression.

When a parent is negative or absent (emotionally or physically), a young child may not have the means to, or may not know how to, express his or her anger to the parent. Because you're a "safer" authority figure in the child's life, he or she may vent that hostility in your direction.

This child needs extra love and understanding. Getting to know the child's home situation may help you to see what's lacking in the child's life. It will also give you the patience and understanding you need to deal graciously with the problem.

Jesus and the Children

We teachers have a role model. God didn't leave us in the dark; he gave us a life-size visual aid in the form of his Son, Jesus Christ. Jesus welcomed interaction with children, and he had a lot to say about them. Jesus never considered children to be an inconvenience. Instead, he used them as living object lessons:

> Then the people brought their little children to
> Jesus so he could put his hands on them and pray for
> them. His followers told them to stop, but Jesus said,
> "Let the little children come to me. Don't stop them,
> because the kingdom of heaven belongs to people who
> are like these children." After Jesus put his hands on
> the children, he left there (Matthew 19:13-15).

Even Jesus' disciples had to learn the importance their master placed on children! On another occasion, Jesus used a child as an example of how adults should relate to God and to each other:

> At that time the followers came to Jesus and asked,
> "Who is greatest in the kingdom of heaven?" Jesus
> called a little child to him and stood the child before his
> followers. Then he said, "I tell you the truth, you must
> change and become like little children. Otherwise, you

will never enter the kingdom of heaven. The greatest
person in the kingdom of heaven is the one who makes
himself humble like this child. Whoever accepts a child
in my name accepts me" (Matthew 18:1-5).

How different Jesus' attitude toward children is when compared to the attitude of many of our churches and much of society! Rather than seeing children as inconvenient, bothersome baggage, Jesus cherished children. And that's exactly what we need to do.

Seven Strategies for Success in the Classroom

We want to love children as Jesus did. We want to disciple them and help them establish strong relationships with the Lord. We want our classrooms to be filled with happy kids full of energy, excitement, and enthusiasm that's focused on the lesson. But so often in the midst of trying to accomplish these noble goals, we trip over our own feet!

Below, we've outlined seven proven strategies that will help you find success in the classroom. Let's take a look.

Strategy 1: Respect and Expect

Jesus taught that a childlike faith is the requirement for entry into heaven. Like Jesus, we need to respect children's faith as well as the children themselves.

> Respecting children is the first step toward creating
> a positive classroom and minimizing discipline issues.

Unfortunately, it's easy to fall into a rut of making negative comments and considering these comments to be discipline. Our weekday preschool playground is a few yards from the back door of my (Gordon's) office. Recently, when I had the door open to let in fresh, crisp afternoon air, I overheard one teacher using a harsh tone as she scolded: "Stop that! That's bad. Your hands are bad. You're crying like a baby." What really caught my attention was that she kept repeating these remarks, which signified to me that the child was not responding at all.

Putting the child down did not result in the kind of behavior the teacher desired. This style of "discipline" will eventually destroy a child's self-image. When we respect children, we curb the demeaning comments that can come out of our mouths all too quickly.

● **Accept and value each child.**
Respect implies recognition, esteem, or worth, with or without

liking, according to Thorndike and Barnhart. Now there's a challenge! We are not required to approve of bad behavior or even to like every child in our classrooms, but we are commanded to love each of them! Giving love and respect, even when a child is not particularly likable, gives children the same sense of worth that Jesus placed on them. Kids immediately recognize whether an adult values them or not, and their behavior inevitably changes accordingly!

As you deal with wrong behavior, make sure that it's clear you value the child. One tried-and-true strategy is the 30/30 method. Give the child thirty seconds of explanation about what was wrong with his or her behavior and how he or she can modify it next time. Then immediately follow up with thirty seconds of telling the child how much God loves him or her and how much you love him or her.

Children need to hear your words of acceptance and approval. As a Sunday school teacher, you are the representation of God's grace to each child. When we correct children, it's vitally important that they feel secure in our unconditional love. We want them to hear between the lines: "I may not like what you are doing, but I love you; and nothing you can do will change my love for you."

● Provide positive expectations.

Because kids want to please their parents and teachers, they intuitively look for the expectations of the adults around them. Many children are hungry for your love and attention—they're only waiting for you to spell out what would put that smile on your face! Even students who constantly challenge your patience will respond to you if you will only tell them how great you expect the day to be. But if kids sense that you don't respect them and don't expect them to behave well, their actions will match your low expectations. If, however, you consistently communicate high respect, both verbally and nonverbally, children will strive to live up to your expectations. To put it simply, if you expect great things from your kids, that's what you're likely to get!

"If Jesus already paid for my sins,
how come I gotta stand in the corner for being bad?"

When a particular student tries your patience, pray for that child throughout the week. Ask God to prepare your heart to love the child and to give you hope that next Sunday's class might be better. Then meet the child at the classroom door before class and verbalize your enthusiasm. You might say: "I'm so glad you're here today, Joey. I just know that we're going to have a great morning. You're going to be such a helper and a kind friend to the other boys and girls in the class. I've prayed for you every day this week because I was so looking forward to seeing you!" Now, these must be honest statements, or the child will see through the hypocrisy. But that's one reason you spend the week praying for him!

A favorite cartoon of ours shows Dennis the Menace sitting at the dinner table with his mother and father. The caption reads: "I am payin' attention. But I listen better if you're saying something nice about me." Isn't this true of all of us? If we are treated well, we respond well. That leads us to the next strategy of good discipline.

Strategy 2: Meet Kids' Needs

When kids are happy and their emotional needs are satisfied, they're more patient with themselves and others and they deal with challenges, frustrations, and pretty much everything else just a little bit better. When kids are emotionally distraught, they simply don't cope with life as well. If you're a parent, you've probably seen this in your own child. In fact, adults function in much the same way. But because kids have little life experience to draw on, the effect of unsettled emotions is magnified.

All sorts of things can drain a child's emotions. It's easy to pick up on this in young children. If a baby is tired or hungry, it fusses. If a child hasn't gotten much attention from Mom or Dad lately, that child may well act out in order to get attention because negative attention seems better than none at all. If there has been a crisis in the family, the child is even more likely to be angry or irritated when he or she encounters life's bumps and bruises.

What do children really need emotionally? They need to know that they're loved and cared for. In his book *Understanding People,* Lawrence J. Crabb says this about the needs of children:

> Children, I suspect, would become more manageable and infinitely more lovable if parents would answer, properly and with some consistency, a few elementary questions that all kids ask. First, "Am I loved?" Correct answer: "Yes, deeply—and here's the unmistakable evidence of my rich, committed involvement with you." Second, "Can I get my own

way?" Correct answer: "No, not without cost—and here is a sample of the painful consequences that result from bucking against God's plan."

These truths apply to the children in your classroom as well.

Emotionally, children are healthiest when they have clear boundaries and evidence of unconditional love when they cross those boundaries.

● **Children need boundaries.**

Years ago, researchers observed children on an elementary school playground. Over a period of several days, the kids' behavior was consistent: they used the entire playground and roamed freely within the cyclone fence. They frequently played right along the fenced boundary of the playground.

The researchers then made an unusual request of the school's administrators. They asked that they be permitted to remove the fence that kept children inside the playground. Teachers were nervous about this request. Since the children were in the habit of playing close to the fence, they assumed that removing the barricade would result in children wandering off the school campus.

When the authorities agreed to have the fence removed, the children's resulting behavior surprised the teachers. Children did not leave the campus. In fact, kids no longer played at the edges of the campus. Instead, they huddled in the middle of the playground, far away from the perceived danger of the limitless edge and close to the security of their teachers. Kids will not tell us this in so many words, but they truly want and need boundaries.

● **Children need to understand consequences.**

Children also need to experience breaking limits and then receiving the forgiveness of a loving adult. As a child, Roger was the overly compliant type. He rarely, if ever, defied parents or teachers. We would all love to have this type of child in our classrooms, but this is exactly the type of child that we should be concerned about.

Never crossing the boundaries, experiencing consequences, and receiving forgiveness prevents a child from knowing that he is loved and accepted unconditionally. This pattern made Roger well-liked by teachers but never very secure about being loved and accepted for who he was. Always being "good" leads a child to believe that love is conditional upon his performance. This child is likely to become an emotionally insecure, perfectionistic adult.

Strategy 3: Walk Your Talk

All too often, we ask kids to behave one way while the teenage and adult workers in the room are behaving in just the opposite way. We often observe frustrated teachers trying to get preschoolers to sit down on the floor during a Bible story while other adults are sitting behind the kids in chairs. The children get a mixed message. To preschoolers, adults "never" do anything wrong. So sitting in chairs must be OK. Everyone gets frustrated!

In elementary classes, we will ask kids to be quiet and listen to the speaker, only to have other adults stand in the back of the room and talk. Which is the child to follow, the spoken rule or the example set by adult leaders?

We heard a great story from an elementary music teacher who had reached her boiling point and exploded at her kids. Recognizing her error, she proceeded to put herself in the time-out chair! That day the children in her class gained a very clear understanding of the rules, and they learned that the consequences for breaking the rules apply to everyone!

You will always have children who, for a variety of reasons, act out more than others. How would you feel about going to Sunday school if your name got called and you received correction at least twenty-five times each week?

A merciful way to deal with a child who is frequently a problem is to gently prompt the entire class. You can refocus the children on the task at hand and away from the distraction without drawing attention to the individual. For example, if Sarah is giggling and whispering while you're explaining the rules of a Bible-learning game, you might say: "I know that you're all going to enjoy this game. But in order to enjoy it, you'll need to know how to play. So right now you need to pay attention to me. You'll have a chance to talk in just a couple of minutes." This is a win-win technique. You gently remind the whole class about proper behavior while sparing one child from repeated negative attention.

● **Offer clear reasons for the rules.**

Remember when you were little and your dad asked you to do something? Sometimes you asked him "Why?" and received the answer, "Because I told you so, that's why!" Do you remember how frustrated you felt with that adult power play?

We teachers often demonstrate that same attitude in the classroom. And while we don't always have to explain our reasons to a child, we must always have clearly formulated reasons for our rules. If we can't state the reason for a rule, it's time to rethink the rule's validity and purpose—and we need a better reason than simply that a certain behavior bugs us!

Time taken to explain the rules is time well spent. Kids generally respond well to thoughtful explanations of your reasoning. And when your rules are based on biblical guidelines, this discussion becomes valuable teaching time.

● Use Scripture appropriately.

Be ready with Scriptures that will motivate your students to demonstrate good behavior, but don't use the Bible as a club to get your way with kids. We've learned that this will frequently backfire! A pastor friend of ours related this incident that happened when his son was very young. The boy was misbehaving, so his father said: "David, don't you know that the Bible says children are to obey their parents? You're supposed to honor your father and mother." The young child responded, "Yes, Daddy, and it also says, 'Fathers, do not exasperate your children.' " Zing!

When you explain biblical standards of behavior to students, be sure they understand that God expects this behavior from kids and adults alike, not just in the classroom, but in life in general. These well-known Bible passages are especially helpful for discussing behavioral standards with the kids in your class.

● **The Golden Rule**—*Do to others what you want them to do to you (Matthew 7:12a).*

Children can understand this rule. They know how they would like to be treated and can easily see how others would like to be treated in the same way.

● **The Greatest Commandment**—*Jesus answered, " 'Love the Lord your God with all your heart, all your soul, and all your mind.' This is the first and most important commandment. And the second commandment is like the first: 'Love your neighbor as you love yourself' " (Matthew 22:37-39).*

Explain to the children that if they are always loving to God and to other people, they will never do anything (on purpose) to hurt anyone. If I love my fellow student, I won't steal his book or ruin her craft project. If I love my teachers, I'll listen to their instructions. If I love God, I won't be silly during prayer time.

● **The Importance of Forgiveness**—*Yes, if you forgive others for their sins, your Father in heaven will also forgive you for your sins. But if you don't forgive others, your Father in heaven will not forgive your sins (Matthew 6:14-15).*

Children have difficulty forgiving other kids, and unforgivingness can multiply classroom problems. Sometimes we need to remind our students that when God forgives us, he forgets all the wrong things we've done and that God expects us to do the same for people who need our forgiveness. You can model this behavior by verbalizing your own forgiveness in front of the class when your students know that you've been annoyed by their behavior.

Strategy 4: Provide Choices

If you're like most adults, you wouldn't take too kindly to arriving at your adult Sunday school class only to discover that everyone in the class was expected to sing a solo that morning as part of the lesson. Neither might you appreciate being told that you had to write a poem that would later be read aloud to the whole class.

But if you were given the choice of singing a solo or writing a poem and if you sing like some of us do, choosing the poem would be a delight! If you were given the added choice of having the poem read aloud or keeping it to yourself, that option might become even more attractive. Being allowed to choose helps kids and adults feel more in control and thus more willing to invest themselves in the task they choose.

If you let kids make choices whenever possible, they'll be happier and will behave better. Making good choices is an important part of the learning process and the discovery of life's natural consequences. If children choose one activity, that means they can't do the other. Allowing kids to make choices teaches them to take responsibility for their actions and to think through the ramifications of their decisions.

Providing choices doesn't necessarily mean that you have to come to class with a briefcase full of diverse activities. You can offer multiple choices within a single activity. For instance, if kids are working on an art project, you might let them choose between markers, crayons, or colored pencils. Offer a variety of papers. Let kids choose to use predrawn workbook pictures or to draw their own pictures. If they're creating a story, let them write it, draw it, or record it. Always be on the lookout for simple ways to let kids choose.

● **Choices lead to consequences, not punishment.**

The use of choice helps kids see that classroom discipline is a matter of consequences rather than punishment. Make it clear to the children that consequences are a given—the choice is how the child decides to behave.

After Andy throws a block and is removed from the block center, be sure to ask him, "Who chose to throw that block?" After he responds, remind him that he knew the rule was that anyone who misuses a toy loses the privilege of playing with that toy for the rest of the day. Reinforce the choice and the consequence by asking, "Since you chose to throw the block, who was it that chose to not play with blocks for the rest of the day?"

When you deal with wrong behaviors in this way, you take yourself out of the role of the bad guy. Andy learns that he is the one who is responsible for his behavior and that the choice not to play with blocks was his—not yours.

The next step is to give Andy some new choices—ones that aren't necessarily bad news! You might say, "Since playing with blocks is no longer an option, would you like to use the art supplies correctly or would you like to play nicely in the housekeeping center?" Andy needs to be reinvolved in the learning process as quickly as possible, both for his sake and for the sake of the other students.

But what if Andy isn't ready to cooperate? What if he simply decides that he doesn't want to do anything? First, encourage him to join in. Point out the fun that other children are having. If Andy remains stubbornly reticent, you might say, "I need to know if you want to participate in today's class. If you'd rather not, you may sit quietly by the wall. If you choose to join in, I expect your cooperation." This effectively eliminates the distraction that Andy is causing and allows the other students to focus on their activities instead of on Andy. And it clearly spells out your expectations for Andy, whether he chooses to sit out or to rejoin the group.

Strategy 5: Give Each Child Focused Attention

If you grew up in the church, think back and recall your Sunday school teachers. Can you remember anything they told you? Probably not. On the other hand, you're likely to retain a strong impression of those teachers as people, either positive or negative.

I remember George well. He was my Sunday School teacher when I was a sophomore in high school. He scared me. He talked about a lot of things that I didn't want to hear. He never connected with me—and never taught me anything that truly impacted my life.

I also remember Terry and his wife. They taught the senior class. My clearest memory is of a time Terry and I took a walk together during a weekend retreat. During that walk, I talked with Terry about things that were on my heart. Terry listened to me—he really listened. I learned that I wanted to be the kind of friend to others that Terry was to me. It wasn't what I learned from Terry in the classroom that had the greatest effect on me—it was what I learned from his friendship.

● **Impart Christian values.**

In his book *How to Really Love Your Child,* practicing pediatric psychiatrist Dr. Ross Campbell states:

> One of the chief complaints we hear from teenagers today is the failure of their parents to give them

ethical or moral standards to live by. This yearning is expressed by older children in many ways. One adolescent says he needs a "meaning in life." Another wants a "standard to guide her." Other seeking youngsters long for "higher guidance," "something to hold on to," or "something to show me how to live." These desperate cries do not come from a few unhappy, discontented teenagers. Most adolescents are feeling and expressing these yearnings.

How does this surprising piece of information impact us as children's workers? Somehow we need to find a way to go beyond teaching the Bible as a collection of facts. We need to teach biblical values and teach them in such a way that children will want to apply these values to their lives. One way to really be effective at imparting values is the way Terry did it—through personal example and focused attention. Terry formed a relationship with me, and because of that relationship, I learned.

Dr. Campbell tells us how kids learn values:

A child first looks to his parents for direction that enables him to develop healthy values. Whether he finds what he needs from his parents depends on two things. The first is whether the parents have it themselves. The second is whether a child can identify with his parents in such a way as to incorporate and accept parental values. A child who does not feel loved will find this difficult.

As children's workers in the church, our role is to assist parents in discipling and nurturing their children. In that role, we must also be aware of the relationship dynamics. To impart values, we must first live them ourselves and then we must have a loving relationship with the child whose life we hope to impact. The content of what we teach in our classrooms is important but not as important as our personal relationships with the children.

As teachers, we are not ready to assume any role in the life of a child until we first have a strong, growing relationship of loving obedience to God. Too many of us give in to the temptation to skip church to work in our classrooms or to skip an adult Bible study because we need to prepare our next lesson. We are doers. But we'll fail if we neglect to fill our own spiritual tanks! Our only hope of impacting lives is to nurture ourselves spiritually and then to nurture caring relationships with our kids.

● Feelings impact learning.

The bottom line is this: How children feel about class affects how and what they learn. In fact, a child's feelings about a Sunday school class will last much longer than the memory of Bible-story facts. In the Sunday school class, we need to be aware of how kids are feeling. As you're teaching, monitor your students' responses. After class, ask yourself these questions:

✓ Was this class a pleasant or unpleasant experience for the children?

✓ Were they excited about what they were learning?

✓ Did I treat each child with respect, kindness, and concern?

✓ Could they make the connection between the lesson and real life?

✓ Did I (or another adult or student) refrain from saying anything that might have been taken as criticism, humiliation, or a put-down?

Self-evaluation is a great tool for becoming a better teacher. You may even want to have a trusted coworker visit your class and then go over the above questions with you. It may feel a bit risky, but there's no better way to discover just how you're coming across to the kids.

● Love your students.

Whether we're relating to our own children at home or to a classroom full of other people's kids, we know that lessons taught without love will be rejected. Taken to its logical conclusion, this principle teaches us that disciplining children out of anger may be worse than not disciplining them at all. If kids feel hostility from us, we're actually encouraging them to reject our instruction—and we're definitely doing more harm than good. That's an alarming thought.

We may have the best intentions of showing love and respect to our students. But if we did not grow up in homes, churches, and schools with adults who knew how to show love and connect with us in meaningful ways, we're at a distinct disadvantage.

Here's some practical help. Campbell gives us four simple communication tools that most kids understand and receive as love:

✓ giving a child meaningful, pleasant eye contact;

✓ giving appropriate physical contact;

✓ planning for times of focused attention; and

✓ using appropriate discipline techniques.

● Use eye contact.

Eye contact is the primary means of conveying unconditional love to children. Unfortunately, when we discipline children (just as when we argue with our spouses), we tend to use our eyes to show disapproval. Removing eye contact is a powerful tool for communicating anger. Just as we can bless with our eyes, we can also condemn.

When our oldest daughter was a toddler, she would crawl up into her daddy's lap and stare into his eyes for an eternity. Her favorite position was nose to nose. When he would bring work home from the office, she would wedge her way between Daddy and the brief-case just enough to grab onto his cheeks (as only a toddler can do) and pull his head into position for the "stare down."

Because small babies' eyes roam around the room, it was once thought that they were unable to focus their eyes on a specific object for the first several months after birth. We now know that they can focus and are, in fact, looking for another set of eyes to stare into! What does this say about the importance of the caregivers in our church nurseries and the power of the relationship that can be built even while changing a diaper?

When you discipline a child, it's vitally important to maintain pleasant eye contact throughout the correction process and into a debriefing time when you restate your love for the child. Just as when Jesus died on the cross and God had to look away from him as he became sin, the pain of the punishment is never as great as the pain of losing the relationship and the intimacy of unconditional love.

As you work with children in your classroom, be sure to get down to their eye level. Realize that an abundance of pleasant eye contact will help the child feel loved. When you give this kind of positive attention from the moment kids arrive in class, you'll erase kids' need to be disruptive in order to gain your negative attention as class goes on.

Frequently take time to pull children aside from the large group to talk one-on-one. This is the best arena for dealing with discipline problems. If kids have experienced your personal, eye-level attention for positive communication, a similar encounter for correction won't be so intimidating.

● **Give appropriate physical contact.**

Besides personal eye contact, both boys and girls need frequent physical affection in order to truly feel loved. Unfortunately, in today's society we must be extremely careful how we touch children. Besides not wanting to make a child uncomfortable, we must be aware of other people's impressions as they watch us interact with children.

Be sure there are always two adults in every classroom—both for your own protection and to give you the freedom to be more affec-tionate with children. With other people's kids, we suggest that you limit your touch to the "bony" areas of the body, including the shoul-ders, the elbows, and the skull. These tend to be seen and under-stood as less intimate areas of our bodies. I (Gordon) like to squeeze the back of older elementary-aged boys' necks. It isn't as "mushy" for them, and the neck is a "safe" zone of the body. One time a student said, "Ouch, you always squeeze so hard!" I apologized and said I wouldn't do it anymore. His response was priceless: "Oh, no. Please keep doing it. I like it!"

Make sure that your touch is quick, not lingering, and that you do it in the open. In your caution, don't give the appearance that you're hiding anything. The more open your display, the more obvious it becomes that your action is innocent. You will be safe, and children will actually appreciate it if you gently hit a shoulder or a knee to show your affection. While sitting at a table with a group of children, you can guide a student's behavior or affirm a student by simply reaching across the table and squeezing his or her hand.

● **Plan focused attention.**

Finally, even in the busyness of a classroom setting, teachers can show their love to children by planning for times of focused attention. This is the hardest of Campbell's suggestions to carry out, because it takes time and planning. Campbell defines focused attention as letting the child know that he or she is the most important person in the world to you at that moment.

When our first child was born, I (Gordon) was teased regularly at church because (so I am told) all I ever talked about was my daughter. But when I thought more about it, I realized how absolutely correct it was for a new little baby to have the fullest attention and focused love of both a mother and a father (and even better, four grandparents!).

Take advantage of those moments before class when the first one or two children arrive early or after class when kids are waiting for late parents, and lavish those kids with focused attention.

Other ways of giving focused attention take a little bit of creativity. Create a bulletin board for the "star of the week." Arrange for a parent to bring in pictures of the "star" as well as the child's favorite snack to share with the class. Call one or two children at home on Saturday each week. Send personal notes in the mail—kids love to get their own mail! Study your lesson well enough so that you can actually put your notes down and look into the eyes of one child at a time as you teach!

The older your students, the more time they'll require to warm up to you. Be positive, but give your older elementary students time to trust that your focused attention is real and pleasant. Children who haven't received much meaningful love at home will have even more trouble accepting it from you. Be patient and persistent. You may be the only one who loves them in such practical ways that they can receive your love, accept your discipline, and allow you to guide them toward knowing, loving, and following Jesus!

Many of us try to give things as a substitute for personal attention. But kids simply aren't at their best unless they're secure in knowing that they are loved, and that requires time and energy spent focusing our attention on them. Every one of God's children deserves to have someone who is irrationally positive about him or her!

Strategy 6: Give Kids Their Wings

In the nursery, babies are dependent upon the teacher for every aspect of their health, safety, care, and nourishment. A class of young toddlers requires a similar level of vigilance. One- and two-year-olds must not be allowed to learn the natural consequences of sticking objects into electrical outlets!

But as a child grows and matures, the teacher's role changes. We must gradually step back and allow children greater freedom to choose and to fail. By letting children take appropriate risks, we encourage them to build relationships with God that are independent of parents' and teachers' faith. It's difficult to watch a child make a bad decision and have to pay the consequences. But it's much more difficult to watch teenagers make foolish life and death decisions because they lacked the opportunity to make choices when they were younger and the consequences of their choices weren't so devastating.

As children move from the nursery into the young-adult world, our role as teachers changes from complete authority figure to guide, mentor, and brother or sister in Christ. Teachers who fail to "give kids their wings" at the appropriate time will foster resentment and rebellion. Teachers who wisely step back from the role of authority figure to that of mentor and friend will build cherished, life-changing relationships with their students.

Strategy 7: Take Joy!

It's no use worrying about whether you'll have discipline problems in your classroom—you will! Gallup polls consistently show that both teachers and parents consider discipline to be one of the top problems in American schools today.

According to the September 1996 Gallup Poll commissioned by Phi Delta Kappa, discipline ranks consistently high as the answer to this question: "What do you think are the biggest problems with which the public schools in this community must deal?"

> This year "drug abuse" edged "lack of discipline"—
> 16% to 15%—as the most frequently mentioned
> "biggest problem" facing local public schools. This
> finding may be somewhat misleading, however,

since a number of the problem categories relate to student control and behavior. If "lack of discipline" and "fighting, violence, and gangs"—the second- and third-place responses—are grouped into a general "control" category, it would reach 29%.

From 1969 to 1985, every poll but one ranked lack of discipline as the top problem. It is interesting that problems related to such critical matters as curriculum, quality of the teaching staff, and the academic performance of students never make it to the top of the list.

So if trained, professional teachers struggle with classroom discipline, take heart—you're not alone!

When teachers voice discouragement with discipline problems, encourage them to look at the problem behaviors as clues. When a child misbehaves, he is telling you that he needs more love or more eye contact; she is asking for more touch or more focused attention. When kids act out, they're giving you a road map to guide you toward what you need to teach them in order to help them be successful in life!

Discouragement happens—don't give up. God has called you to be a discipler of kids, not just a teacher of lessons! You'll discover precious rewards in the process of nurturing and discipling children when you

- respect and expect,
- meet kids' needs,
- walk your talk,
- provide choices,
- give each child focused attention,
- give kids their wings, and
- take joy!

Take joy when you know that each child in today's class felt your love and approval. Take joy when you've met the emotional needs of a hurting child. Take joy when a child who was closed and distrustful gives you her trust. Take joy when a child who acted out accepts the logical consequences of his behavior without protest. Take joy when you see that children have gained more than just facts from your lesson. Take joy each time you see a child take a step toward developing a personal relationship with God. Take joy when you see your students embracing and living out the Christian values you've modeled. Take joy, knowing that you've helped the children in your class learn to know, love, and follow Jesus.

2 Kids Will Be Kids!

t's a rare child who acts out for no apparent reason. In their emotional and social immaturity, children misbehave when they seek to meet their own needs in ways that are inappropriate or hurtful to others. In the discipline process, we help children learn to meet their needs in appropriate ways or to withhold gratification until their desires can be fulfilled at an acceptable time.

The more we teachers (and parents) understand about the needs of children at various ages, the more we can anticipate an individual child's behavior. Parents naturally understand that a baby needs food, sleep, and changing frequently throughout each day. And we plan time to allow for the frequent interruptions children's needs impose on our daily schedules. We make allowances for a baby who cries in order to get fed—something we would find socially incorrect in our adult friends.

As children grow through various developmental stages, their needs and desires change. At each stage we need to be proactive in heading off discipline problems by adapting our teaching and disciplining methods to meet the needs of the children we serve.

> When we understand the children we are teaching, we can better anticipate their problem behaviors, develop realistic expectations, and set up classroom systems to meet needs and head off problems before they occur.

In Chapter 1 we discussed the principle that all children behave better when their physical and emotional needs are met. To understand kids, we need to be aware of the emotional health of their families. To help them, we must adapt our expectations of children who are emotionally needy. Annie may be having difficulty at school; Tony's parents may be divorcing. Instead of being frustrated with Annie and Tony, the wise teacher will provide an extra measure of understanding and emotional support.

One characteristic of all children is a limited attention span. The attention span of a concrete-thinking child (from birth to early adolescence) is no more than one minute per year of age. Although a child can focus on a television show or a video for thirty minutes, his or her attention span is actually refocusing every few minutes. *Sesame Street* was developed based on this understanding. An hour-long lesson on a letter, a number, and a principle fits the youngest viewer's attention span because the characters, techniques, sets, and illustrations all change every few minutes.

We'll waste valuable teaching time if we attempt to fight the way God made kids! Instead, let's respect children by taking time to understand them.

Meeting the Needs of Toddlers and Twos

● Ts & 2s: Physical Development

When small children can finally get up and move on their own, the whole world becomes their playground and scientific laboratory. God has programmed toddlers to move, explore, and experience everything that crosses their paths.

The furniture in your toddler classroom must be carefully chosen. Toddlers have little fear of danger and like to climb stairs and chairs on their own. Eliminating dangerous climbers, chairs, and other objects that can tip over when a toddler climbs on them will greatly enhance the safety of your classroom and reduce your stress!

Keep chemicals (spray cleaners, baby lotion) and objects children shouldn't touch on high shelves or in locked cabinets. Cover outlets and remove cords from toddlers' reach. Store toys and materials that children use on low, open shelves so children can find and return the items of their choice.

Some toddlers and twos will be in diapers; others will be transitioning to training pants. Ask parents to provide disposables only. Disposables are more convenient for you, and they will help maintain a healthy environment. Be sure to schedule carefully spaced bathroom breaks for the whole class.

When young children are at church for an extended period of time, you can lessen discipline problems by providing for their physical needs with snacks, outdoor exercise, and nap or rest time. If you have tried and failed to provide a nap time, remember that young children are legalists about schedules. If you repeat the pattern often enough, eventually toddlers won't allow you to skip the same rest period that they previously rejected. Be consistent with your expectations, and don't give up.

● Ts & 2s: Intellectual Development

Young children use all of their senses to the fullest extent in their exploration of the world. Plan to teach toddlers in the way they learn best: they need to see, touch, taste, smell, and hear. Allow them plenty of time to explore—don't rush them from one activity to another.

The toddler's attention span is approximately two minutes. The teacher who's trying to tell a Bible story that lasts several minutes will discover that God has created something in the toddler's body that urges it to "wiggle, wiggle, wiggle!" Between the teacher's will and God's design, guess who wins?

Gordon's first experience with a class of two-year-olds taught him a whole lot about toddlers' need to explore. The curriculum contained a painting activity. After the children started painting, Gordon realized it would have been a good idea to use smocks. He left the room for just a few moments. When he returned with the smocks, he discovered that the white dress with blue polka dots worn by a first-timer now also had pink polka dots. Fortunately the parents decided to keep their child in this class where young children really had fun! Word finally got around that Sunday school was a place for kids to dress in play clothes because the children's pastor valued fun and learning over fashion!

Toddlers are extremely physical. Play is their work! More than at any other age, the toddler's mind and body work together to learn thorough energetic, imaginative play. Choose puzzles and toys that help toddlers learn eye-hand coordination. Choose activities that allow children to experience self-sufficiency as they work to develop a sense of self-reliance. Allow toddlers to do activities as independently as possible and then celebrate their successes.

● Ts & 2s: Emotional Development

Young children need to test limits. Rules, therefore, must be simple and enforceable. Repeating the rules will help children remember them.

Routine helps toddlers understand what is expected. Children will be more comfortable and will behave better when you follow a consistent routine. Familiar surroundings and classroom helpers also reinforce the child's sense of security. It is important to have substitutes fully trained in the way things are done in each room, because toddlers and twos do not easily adjust to new settings.

These little ones will often reflect the emotional state of those around them. Their teacher needs to maintain a calm, gentle spirit.

Bearing in mind that the goal of discipline is to disciple children, remember that young children act out their feelings and thoughts in their play. Provide open-ended activities during which you can learn what's going on inside children's heads. When you offer a house-keeping center, you're providing the setting for children to apply what they've learned and at the same time, you gain a window into the child's heart and home life. By observing and interacting with children in this setting, you can suggest healthy ways for little ones to deal with anger and frustration.

● Ts & 2s: Social Development

These little ones are copycats. If someone in the room takes his or her shoes off, toddlers will think they'd better try that, too! So the wise teacher makes sure that each of the workers in the classroom consistently models the preferred behavior. If the kids should not toss blocks and dolls, classroom helpers should also refrain from tossing them—even if they're just tossing the blocks back into the bin as they're cleaning up.

The realistic teacher understands that toddlers and twos must constantly relearn what acceptable behavior is. Be ready to repeat rules and positively redirect children constantly throughout the session. Children at this age will frequently invade other children's activities and demonstrate bossy, selfish behavior. They should be encouraged to share but not expected to do so on their own. They engage primarily in solitary play. This is one of the several stages that God has designed to help children learn independence. Lessons should allow for a wide variety of choices for these youngest learners.

● Ts & 2s: Spiritual Development

Build into your classroom regular times for individual attention and hugs. Your attention will not only help toddlers behave better—it will actively create for the child a picture of Jesus as someone who cares for him or her. Key biblical concepts for toddlers and twos include "God cares for you" and "God made everything," so be ready to get on your hands and knees to explore the world with this child!

To be at their best, toddlers needs loads of adult attention, praise, and encouragement in a safe, secure world of familiar people and routines.

Meeting the Needs of Preschoolers

● Preschool: Physical Development

Because these children have started to master control of their large-muscle groups, they seem to be constantly in motion. They need to move and exercise those large muscles, but they tire easily. They may look like they need to "get the wiggles out" when what they truly need is to rest. (Do not expect them to sleep at nap time, though.) Too much activity leaves preschoolers overstimulated. Exercising a tired three- or four-year-old will create more discipline problems, since motion releases adrenaline that the child will seek to use up.

Preschoolers are beginning to use the small muscles of their hands. They enjoy being given opportunities to draw and cut. By age four, children are gaining a certain amount of control over fine motor-skills and enjoy using scissors more frequently. Success breeds good behavior, so make sure that art projects do not frustrate your children. At this age, children should be allowed to do most of their own cutting, primarily on predrawn, heavy, straight lines. Avoid small details and projects with lots of curves and angles. Provide large crayons and large paintbrushes that are easily manipulated, and do not expect children to fill in coloring book-type pictures. Children will be more satisfied and more creatively challenged if they work on blank sheets of paper.

One characteristic of preschoolers that tends to fray a teacher's nerves is their tendency to be noisy and boisterous. Teachers we know have commented that preschoolers have only one kind of voice—the kind that's not intended for indoor use! You'll need to help them lower the decibel level. Call attention to your own quiet, calm voice to demonstrate what kind of volume is appropriate in the classroom.

● Preschool: Intellectual Development

Four-year-olds are beginning to "read" pictures. They enjoy looking at a variety of books and making up stories to go with the pictures. They have wonderful imaginations, and their stories tend to be full of exaggeration. Be careful not to suggest that they're lying. Instead, compliment their creative genius and congratulate them on making up wonderful stories!

Do help children distinguish between fantasy and reality. When these children tell stories, it's sometimes hard for adults to discern what's real and what's imagined. Offer clarification by reminding children that Bible stories are "really true" and that stories about superheroes are just make-believe. We like to promise parents that we'll believe only half of what we hear about them if they'll believe only half of what they hear about us! One time we were talking about helpers, like policemen, when four-year-old twins said a "helper" made their daddy stop that morning on the way to church!

Preschoolers will participate in an activity only for the duration of their interest. At this stage the average attention span will be a mere three to four minutes. This does not mean that you can't tell a ten-minute Bible story, however. To keep a young child involved in a single activity, change the focus within the activity. Visuals, questions, movement, and active participation can all keep children interested beyond the brief initial frame of their attention span.

Children at this age need to share their ideas. Plan plenty of time for them to respond to and "discuss" the Bible lesson. Slow down—be careful not to pack your lessons too full of teacher talk. These children are eager to "help" tell the story.

Also be ready for these kids to make up nonsense words and to tell nonsense jokes. Four-year-olds are developing a new wealth of vocabulary words and social abilities. Rather than becoming annoyed, be ready to laugh and enjoy their silly, age-appropriate humor!

Four-year-olds are notorious for asking "Why?" Teachers (and parents) need to be patient with these inquisitive minds because the willingness of adults to answer questions at this stage will have a direct impact on children's willingness to ask questions when they reach early adolescence. One technique for challenging the child's mind and preserving your own is to respond to the child's question with a question of your own: "Why do you think?"

Preschoolers may well lack the language skills and vocabulary to actually converse, so they need you to listen patiently and help them communicate their ideas. You'll often hear four-year-olds say, "I don't know," when, in fact, they do know—they just don't know that they know. Kids at this age have been accumulating knowledge at an incredible rate. But that knowledge isn't completely organized and classified. If you're asking a question that a student does know the answer to, help the child by saying: "Yes, I think you do know. Remember when we talked about...?" This simple statement will often direct the child's brain to the knowledge that he or she already has, but could not otherwise retrieve.

Preschoolers can and will follow simple instructions when you give no more than two or three commands at a time. Give your instructions in short bursts and then wait for children to respond and complete one or two steps before you announce the next set of instructions. Praise your students for each completed step. If kids seem frustrated and "ornery," do a quick self-check: Are my instructions clear? Am I asking them to do too many things at once? Am I giving them enough coaching so they can approach the task with confidence?

Preschoolers learn primarily by the example of adults. Therefore, wise teachers model the behavior they want the children to imitate. If children are to sit on the floor during the story, the adults need to sit on the floor. If children should be quiet while the teacher talks, other classroom helpers should, too.

● **Preschool: Emotional Development**

Unlike two-year-old children who are in a "leaving" cycle, preschoolers are entering a "cleaving" cycle. They especially want to please adults. They're eager to help the teacher, so give them lots of opportunities to be classroom "helpers." They have a strong need for appreciation, so be sure to thank them specifically for being helpful and kind. It's great to let them to do their own cleanup—with coaching and assistance from you, of course! Children who take responsibility for their own things feel good about themselves and about their contributions to the class. This positive self-feedback will lead to better behavior.

At this stage of development, children exhibit emotions freely and intensely. Our own daughter can change from smiles to screams with a snap of the fingers. Again, adults need to model and coach appropriate emotional responses. These kids are like mirrors—they'll often give back exactly what they see. The four-year-old boy who gets dropped off by an apprehensive parent will arrive reflecting the fear of his mother. The lighthearted teacher will generally have more carefree students.

● Preschool: Social Development

Three- and four-year-olds are beginning to develop a sense of group identity, but they interpret the whole in terms of themselves. In other words, they will be watching to see that everyone in the group receives equal and fair treatment. Rules must be enforced consistently, and rewards and privileges should be dispensed evenly.

Expect preschoolers to engage in "parallel" play: two children will play side by side but will have little true interaction. (It is best at this age to have multiple toys of the same type!) Casual observers might think that children are playing together, when in reality, they are doing similar activities right next to each other.

Although they will share some things at this age, preschoolers are still naturally focused on themselves. It's unrealistic to expect them to be unselfish, no matter how much we would like them to be.

Teachers will still need to frequently identify and define sharing while overlooking a certain amount of selfishness. Teachers also need to be ready for the "bully" game. Three-year-olds like to pretend to be the "bad guy." Be careful not to step in and discipline what is healthy play (pretending in a make-believe game), but be prepared to stop what is not (actually bullying other children)!

● Preschool: Spiritual Development

Modeling is important for teaching biblical concepts. Children need practice interacting and applying Bible truths that have social implications. If one child is unkind to another, stop and take advantage of the teachable moment. Take the child aside and quietly reinforce the Bible truth that God wants us to love one another and that we show love by being kind. Ask how the child can show kindness. Then encourage the child to go back to the activity and show kindness to the child whose feelings were hurt. These are the lessons that will stick with children long after class is over.

Meeting the Needs of Kindergartners

● K: Physical Development

Although kindergartners appear less restless than preschoolers, they are full of energy and need exercise. Allow time for active games and, when appropriate, outdoor play. Because kindergartners have greater coordination and control of large-muscle groups and are more group-oriented, you can effectively introduce games involving the whole class. Adults need to be present to explain and participate in games, to teach good sportsmanship, and to settle kids' concerns about fairness. Game time is also a great time for adults to give personal attention since five-year-olds love to demonstrate their physical skills.

● K: Intellectual Development

A key phrase for the kindergarten child is "Let me do it." Kindergartners are eager to learn, and they learn best and behave best when they're actively involved in the lesson. Although their attention span is now five to six minutes, it only lasts as long as the children are involved and interested in the project or story. Use stories that are full of action, and allow children to give physical and verbal responses. Kindergartners especially enjoy completing stories. When children are involved in the telling, a Bible story can be repeated over and over without losing their attention and interest.

Memorization is not necessarily a good thing for five-year-olds. Although they have good memories, their vocabulary exceeds their ability to understand. They can parrot adult words and sentences with little or no comprehension. Memorization is worthwhile for kindergartners only when they understand what it is they're memorizing.

For successful classroom management, it's important to spell out expectations clearly. Ask, "What does being kind look like? What does it sound like? How can you tell if you're respecting others?" Help students find concrete examples of each behavior that everyone can understand.

At this age, children begin to understand cause-and-effect relationships. Knowing this, a teacher can begin to use stated consequences and incentive programs more effectively. Tools such as time-out chairs, marble jars (see Chapter 4), and class celebrations make sense to five-year-olds. But these children also require a more thorough discussion of why a rule exists than younger children do.

Kindergartners understand time in one-day increments. Everything revolves around the here and now. Rewards and punishment must, therefore, be immediate. Promising a distant reward or threatening a later punishment has little effect or meaning. Tomorrow might as well be next year.

● K: Emotional Development

Many of the happiest teachers we have known work with kindergartners. These children are even more appreciative of adult attention than preschoolers. Kindergartners thrive on praise and will cooperate with significant adults in order to please them and gain approval.

Five-year-olds identify with specific adults and imitate them. Therefore, role models are even more important at this age. As with previous age levels, adults need to model what they want the kids to do by supporting and obeying class rules.

Kindergartners will go to any lengths to gain individual attention. If you do not provide this in your classroom, your students will often resort to bad behavior to achieve their goal. A wise teacher makes sure that good behavior receives attention. Some acting out can be extinguished by simply ignoring it. If the child doesn't get the desired reaction from the teacher, he or she may decide that an action is not worth repeating.

Teachers need to be ready to deal with kindergartners' fragile emotions. Although they'll have less frequent outbursts and more appropriate expression of emotion than younger children, kindergartners also make lightning-quick changes from one mood to another. We saw this with our own child who would often follow an angry outburst with "I love you, Mommy." It's fairly common to encounter five-year-olds who are experiencing deep-seated jealousy over the new baby Mom and Dad just brought home. If you know that one of your students has a new baby at home, guide that child to the housekeeping center where he or she can express these emotions in creative play. For many children, having the chance to express emotion in play is all they need in order to process their feelings and become more comfortable in a new situation such as having a new sibling. As you watch children play, be ready to talk to those who are having trouble dealing with strong emotions.

Kindergartners have difficulty determining whether an adult is pretending. Therefore, drama and puppets can be powerful teaching tools. Sarcasm, however, can be extremely destructive. Since these kids always take adults at face value, they may not understand that you're just kidding when you tease or make a sarcastic comment. Praise, instruction, expectations, and correction all need to be stated in simple, concrete, straightforward terms.

Make it a point to greet children as they arrive in class. Get down on their level and give meaningful eye contact as you tell each child how glad you are to see him or her. Again, the proven rule applies: Positive personal attention given early in class will make kids less prone to act out later on in order to provoke your attention.

● K: Social Development

Because children at this age are so conscious of their peers, group dynamics can be used to channel classroom behavior. The kindergarten teacher must be a cheerleader for positive behavior! "Catch" every child doing something good—but avoid pointing out good behavior from the same children over and over.

Kindergartners care passionately about what's fair and what's not fair, and they'll become very upset if they don't receive consistent treatment from adults. Class rules and consequences for breaking them need to be clearly stated. At this age, children are developing problem-solving skills, so you'll want to include them in developing rules and consequences.

Although kindergartners enjoy playing with other children, teachers may find competition to be detrimental. Girls are advancing beyond boys at this age and have a natural advantage in most competitions. Kindergartners have a new understanding of relationships and peers that makes them sensitive to the personal struggles that emerge when there are winners and losers.

● K: Spiritual Development

Spiritually, kindergartners understand God's love as it is demonstrated to them by significant adults. Authority figures help create their concept of God. Therefore, our discipline of these children needs to include affection, love, and forgiveness. Again, the 30/30 rule is a good technique to remember. Start with thirty seconds of telling children who act out what was wrong with their behavior, and always follow with an equal amount of time telling children how much you love them.

Meeting the Needs of the Early-Elementary Child

● 6s & 7s: Physical Development

In early-elementary years, kids are constantly moving. These students are unable to sit still for much more than a few minutes. Teachers will be frustrated if they expect these children to behave correctly during a long, boring lecture or a series of pencil-and-paper activities at a desk. Because they're in the process of developing control of their large-muscle groups, these kids truly are unable to move slowly. Their awkwardness causes them to get dirty easily—it's next to impossible for them to not spill drinks or paint!

Active-learning experiences are a must for your classroom of first- and second-graders. These children need an abundance of room to move freely and a frequent change of focus. Vary the pace of the lesson and the settings in which you teach your kids. Move around the room or even around your church.

● 6s & 7s: Intellectual Development

First- and second-graders are adventurers. In fact, these children learn primarily by experimentation and discovery. This is another reason that active-learning experiences are the preferred teaching method for kids of this age. Design your lessons to offer a variety of activities that fit the interests and abilities of the group, and allow students to make choices about which activities they do. The more adventure you program into your lessons, the more kids will want to participate. They'll stay on task, and you'll avoid discipline problems.

At the same time, these children enjoy a certain measure of repetition and the security that comes from familiar routines. While repetition may become boring for the adult, it gives first- and second-graders the security of mastering an activity. Take care to balance new experiences with familiar ones. Even when several new activities are being introduced, early-elementary classrooms need to stay on a consistent schedule.

In first- and second-grade, kids' listening skills are developing quickly. Don't be fooled into thinking that their attention span is increasing greatly also. It's still only six to eight minutes long, with girls tending to have longer attention spans than boys.

Almost all preschoolers are bodily kinesthetic learners, but auditory learners begin emerging in early-elementary years. You'll find these children better equipped to handle verbal instructions and participate in question and answer times.

"Remember, this is a *church* picnic—so always say 'amen' after you burp!"

First- and second-graders are also quickly expanding their speaking skills. Again, girls will tend to have more conversation skills than boys. These children will enjoy and benefit from an interactive-learning environment in which students discuss the answers to questions in small groups and then share their ideas and applications with the entire class.

First- and second-graders are only beginning to read. Most or all are still sounding out words. When a student is asked to read out loud, other students will have difficulty following what is read one word at a time. The resulting boredom will almost always cause fidgets and other discipline problems. Meanwhile, the reader may feel threatened and act out in order to escape embarrassment.

It's best to avoid singling out kids to read aloud. Instead, do the reading yourself as students follow along, or have the whole class read the passage aloud together. It's extremely helpful to keep in your classroom a set of easy-to-read Bibles such as the New Century Version.

Remember that these children think literally. It's important to give instructions in concrete terms with words kids can easily understand. Consequences must be immediate and practical, since, like kindergartners, these children have a very limited concept of time. The here and now is all that really exists in a first- or second-grader's mind.

Six- and seven-year-olds can learn to sing in tune and clap out rhythms, so music is more fun than ever! A good attention-getting device for this age level is a rhythmic hand-clap signal from the teacher to which all students are trained to respond by clapping back the same rhythm.

● 6s & 7s: Emotional Development

Six- and seven-year-olds desire friendships with adults. Their social and emotional needs are met best by having a consistent staff of teachers and helpers in the classroom. The quality of the teacher-student relationship will greatly impact these kids. They need to be understood and to have a healthy sense of self-worth. A friendship with a significant adult teacher can address both of these needs. Make a point of calling students by name and knowing their likes, dislikes, and special interests.

Encourage your first- and second-graders to do their best and not to be discouraged over imperfection. Because these kids tend to be unrealistic about their expectations of themselves, this is sometimes called the "eraser age." First- and second-graders feel driven to master every skill and every task. Because they're so hard on themselves, they have a deep need for the approval of the adults in their lives.

Be careful not to make comparisons between students' work. Avoid pointing out mistakes or imperfections to the whole group. Be cautious about showing examples of craft projects that have been made by an adult, because these children will compare their own work to that of the teacher and will end up being dissatisfied with what they've done.

Early-elementary children often express their emotions physically, with little control. Be ready to take aside a child whose emotions have gotten out of control. Help the child identify the emotions that are causing the inappropriate behavior and explain that these feelings are OK. Losing control, however, is not OK. Redirect the child to appropriate ways of dealing with strong emotions.

Seven-year-olds tend to be worriers. They are generally thoughtful and introspective and much less likely to take risks than six-year-olds. To account for these needs, allow time for quiet reflection within each lesson. It's best to avoid activities that seem risky—anything that could make a child look foolish in front of his or her classmates. Keep those activities on a strictly volunteer basis. Some of your more outgoing students who enjoy attention and are secure and willing to laugh at themselves may do fine, but most seven-year-olds will not.

● 6s & 7s: Social Development

Expect your six- and seven-year-olds to clamor to be first at everything. Being first is very important for them. Children of this age have difficulty taking turns and need opportunities to practice this social skill. Recognize that you will need to repeat activities so that several kids can be "first." Repeating activities gives security to the children, gives them hope that they will get their turn to be first, and helps them learn to share.

You'll need to help your first- and second-graders learn to be considerate of others. While they're often insensitive to the feelings of their peers, they tend to be hypersensitive about being accepted themselves, especially among their peers.

Teachers can avoid a host of interpersonal problems by reducing or eliminating competitive activities in the classroom. The majority of these children find competition threatening, and they don't cope well with losing. In fact, most early-elementary kids are very poor losers. Never place children in jeopardy of losing over and over again. Defuse competitive activities by setting them up so each child will have a chance to win. Or do away with the competitive part entirely.

Fortunately, almost all kids enjoy cooperative activities. And cooperative activities build real-life skills that will benefit students even into adult life. Students need to learn to work together, to listen to everyone, to accept group decisions, and to play various roles within a group. And everyone enjoys the sense of friendship and accomplishment that cooperative activities provide. You'll make your classroom a happier, more secure place for your students when you reduce competition and emphasize cooperation.

Because these children are becoming socially adept, we sometimes make the mistake of trying to reason with them about how their actions might affect others. This is a difficult transition for most six- and seven-year-olds. Instead, when you're correcting a child, phrase your questions from the child's point of view: "How would you feel if...?" Kids will also benefit from discussion of what "respecting others" looks like and sounds like in your classroom.

● 6s & 7s: Spiritual Development

As concrete thinkers, first- and second-graders have difficulty grasping abstract concepts and symbolism—including religious terms. When you're teaching about difficult concepts such as Communion and baptism, be aware that the majority of six- and seven-year-olds will not be able to grasp these concepts in one sitting. Make your lessons as "hands-on" as possible. For instance, when you're teaching about forgiveness, let children dirty their hands and then wash them in soapy water. As you dry their hands, say, "God loves you and forgives you." Introduce difficult concepts by reducing them to their most concrete level. Recognize the fact that parroting what they've heard you say does not mean that children understand. Be patient. Allow time for children to process these ideas.

In early-elementary years, children's focus can easily "snag" on a specific aspect of a story or situation. Be careful about including difficult concepts or overly stimulating details in your Bible story. Children may fix their focus on that point, stop listening, and miss the rest of the story. For example, when we were telling the story of Jesus' parents fleeing to Egypt, one student kept thinking and rethinking why Joseph would use a donkey to get out of the country fast. Any six-year-old knows you use airplanes for that! He puzzled on that one point and missed the rest of the story. If you see this happening with one of your students, ask the child a question to redirect his attention. For instance, you might ask, "Jamie, why did Jesus' parents have to hurry to Egypt?" Be careful not to embarrass the child—after all, he is focused on the story, just not on the same part of it as the rest of the class!

Some Bible stories can be frightening for kids of this age. At Easter time, for instance, focus on Jesus' love and his willingness to give his life for us. Don't give a graphic description of Jesus' death on the cross, or your students' attention may remain there. Instead, move on to the Resurrection. Leave kids with the message that Jesus' love is stronger than anything and that his victory over death opens the way to heaven.

On the other hand, first- and second-graders love Bible stories that are full of action and dialogue. They enjoy lively participation in stories that capture their imagination. They find it troubling, however, when things don't turn out "fair." If children seem upset with the outcome of a Bible story, take time to explain that even if things seem unfair at this point, we can always trust God to make things turn out right in the end.

Since children of this age derive their understanding of our loving, merciful God largely from their relationships with their own parents, you'll want to make an effort to get to know the families of the students. If Scott's dad walked out on his wife and kids, Scott will be confused and frustrated by the teacher who talks about God, our loving Father. Scott's anger toward his father may well be transferred to the teacher and ultimately, to God. Children like Scott will require an extra measure of attention and grace. Explain to Scott one-on-one that God never leaves us, that God loves us no matter what, and that nothing can separate us from God's love.

Meeting the Needs of the Middle-Elementary Child

● 8s & 9s: Physical Development

Although the majority of girls are still ahead of boys developmentally, both boys and girls at this age can react physically with speed and accuracy. They enjoy organized games and can get involved in larger group activities than before.

● 8s & 9s: Intellectual Development

In third and fourth grades, kids' skills and abilities seem to multiply daily! Their reading and writing skills have advanced to the point where they can work independently for longer periods of time. They enjoy the challenge of more in-depth projects and questions. They'll stick with more complex craft projects, and they'll even start assuming responsibility for cleaning up after themselves!

If some of your students don't match up to this description, remember that almost ten years of training have gone into each child's makeup. What they *can* do and what they have been *trained* to do may be two completely different things. So, while you know that your students are able to work and accept responsibility, don't assume that they have learned to do so. Your role as a discipler is to nurture the students and help them reach their full potential.

You'll have great success with interactive-learning techniques at this age. Allow children to work together in small groups and then display or discuss the outcome of their projects with the whole group. At this stage, children can see possibilities of multiple correct answers and ideas. This type of discussion can lead to research—something the middle-elementary child will likely love.

These children are seldom content to sit still during a traditional passive education experience with heavy emphasis on lecture and work sheets. When kids have been passive too long, expect them to begin acting out. Middle-elementary students are at a peak of creativity. To learn, they need to experience the lesson from many different angles and find a personal way to express what they've discovered.

In the middle years, the child's value system is developing. It is important to this fragile developmental process that these children experience a sense of fair play. Therefore, teachers need to make sure that an atmosphere of trust exists in the classroom. Any hint that an adult does not trust a child at this age may damage the child's self-confidence—and consequently his or her trust in the adult and his or her willingness to be open and honest.

● 8s & 9s: Emotional Development

To be emotionally fulfilled, eights and nines need access to a broad variety of creative, meaningful activities. Art and music help these children internalize information and enhance their self-concepts. Exploring new methods of self-expression enhances kids' creativity, gives them a sense of accomplishment, and encourages healthy self-images. Kids of this age especially enjoy educational games.

It's important for teachers to demonstrate how these new experiences are relevant. These kids will reject activities that are meaningless time-fillers.

It's appropriate to give these children an increased number of responsibilities. At this age level, challenging students to new heights and letting them know that you trust them to do well will result in positive behavior and better attitudes about themselves and the class in general.

God has "wired" these kids to have high expectations of themselves. Rather than chiding them into proper behavior, be a mentor who challenges them, sets high but reasonable goals, and encourages and coaches them to meet the challenge. Your own modeling will set the mark that kids will naturally strive for.

It's not at all unusual for third- and fourth-graders to attempt tasks well beyond their abilities and then become extremely upset when they fail. The usual results are anger, frustration, and bad attitudes. Since these children can be overly self-critical, wise teachers guide them in choosing activities in which they'll experience at least some measure of success.

Eight- and nine-year-olds are developing their identities, largely through the influence of their peers. They look for models, but they look less and less in the adult world. Although their dependence on adults is decreasing, their need for loving support continues, especially since their peers can be rough on them. More than anything, this child is looking for a place to belong.

Most eights and nines can discuss and evaluate their feelings and actions with their peers. They've begun to understand themselves through others. All of this might lead you to believe that they would be open to evaluative criticism from adults as well. However, they have an extremely difficult time accepting evaluation from authority figures. A better plan is to guide discussion between students in small-group settings. Kids' honesty and desire for truth and fairness can be put to work to help them correct and challenge each other. This approach is generally more successful than trying to achieve the same results from the top down.

If you see teasing, put-downs, and criticism in your classroom, you may be observing a child who is venting built-up anger. Being critical of the child's behavior at this point may only make the situation worse. First, see if you can determine what's troubling the child. The child who's acting out may not even realize that he or she is angry. Negative comments should be a red flag to the teacher that something else is going on in the child's life that needs to be addressed.

● 8s & 9s: Social Development

Middle-elementary children are very concerned about the truth. In situations of conflict that call for adult intervention, children on both sides of the conflict will typically feel drawn to tell the teacher what "really" happened regarding the situation. These kids have a strong desire for a clearly developed code of right and wrong and fairness in executing it.

It's still best to avoid highly competitive activities. These children desperately need approval from both their peers and adults. We do not want our kids to feel like "losers" at church. This is especially true in middle-elementary years when children typically place unrealistic expectations on themselves.

At this stage, you may find that you can do more reasoning with the children in discipline situations. They're beginning to understand others' points of view, and can see others' feelings and attitudes. They'll also readily listen to adults and peers. Make sure you give your students opportunities to discuss classroom expectations, rules, and consequences. The group process can strengthen your ability to create and enforce meaningful systems of discipline.

Middle-elementary children will begin to reach out to others and, for the first time, show more concern for others than themselves. They'll enjoy missions projects. They'll be empathetic with people whose rights have been violated or feelings hurt. They have a strong need for mutual acceptance, understanding, and cooperation. Because of these traits, these children can be truly delightful to teach!

Although children at this age are beginning to accept personal limitations and differences in skill levels within their own gender, they may well resent the opposite sex. Boys will be attracted to other boys for friendships, and girls will be drawn to other girls. In fact, for healthy development to take place, these children each need to have a special friend of the same gender.

In your classroom, you will almost certainly experience the "battle of the sexes." The tension between girls and boys in your classroom may lead you to believe that classes should be grouped by gender. However, we have often observed that boys tend to be a little bit more gentlemanly when they're in the presence and under the peer pressure of girls, and girls tend to be a little less silly and critical when boys are around.

Besides, if our goal is to disciple children, interpersonal problems should not be avoided but worked through. We need to deal with the animosity and struggles between students of different genders. It is wise to plan church-related group activities at this age to allow kids to develop social relationships with both sexes.

● 8s & 9s: Spiritual Development

Although they have may difficulty admitting their own wrongdoing, children at this age are able to begin evaluating ethics and actions by biblical standards. Remember, these children are good researchers. Put this strength to use by having the class work together to find Scripture verses to form the framework for your class rules and expectations. A great benefit of doing this is that God becomes the authority—not the teacher!

Most third- and fourth-graders can understand concepts of sin and forgiveness. If they have not already done so, many of them will now desire to become members of God's family. Entering a relationship with God and receiving God's unconditional love satisfies kids' spiritual hunger as well as their need for approval. Children who have made a commitment to follow Jesus will have every reason to be loving and kind in your classroom, and when you need to correct them, their spiritual "antennae" will be alert for guidance from God's Word.

Meeting the Needs of the Late-Elementary/Early-Adolescent Child

Child or Youth?

Schools and churches across America group ten- and eleven-year-olds in a variety of ways. Normally the division between children's ministry and youth ministry and elementary school and middle school or junior high falls either between fifth and sixth grades or between sixth and seventh. We recommend that you group children in your church according to the pattern of the local school district in which most of your students reside.

It's difficult to categorically describe these children because they enter adolescence at different times. In fact, if there is one overarching characteristic of this group of kids, it is that each one is completely unique and is maturing socially, physically, emotionally, mentally, and spiritually at his or her own rate.

With younger kids, experts have learned to predict with some accuracy the onset and rate of each developmental change. Not every child starts walking at exactly the same age, but nearly all of them do it just before or after their first birthday. Puberty, however, may start anywhere within the five-year period of ten to fourteen years of age. And the many changes that puberty involves happen at different rates for each individual, and these changes happen simultaneously within the individual. In other words, the child is changing socially, mentally, physically, and emotionally all at the same time. The changes impact each other and are further complicated by outside influences coming from the student's home, school, church, circle of friends, and the media.

Educational psychologist Donald Eichorn refers to this period of

"I THINK WHAT MRS. NITWHIPPLE IS TRYING TO SAY IS THAT WE NEED HELP WITH THE SIXTH-GRADERS THIS MORNING."

transition between childhood and adolescence as "transescence" and classifies it as a specific, identifiable period of development uniquely different from both childhood and adolescence. It begins just prior to the onset of puberty and continues through the early years of adolescence. It is characterized by dramatic changes in the child's physical development, mental and intellectual functions, and social relationships and interests.

The brave souls who teach these kids need to be sensitive to the vast differences among their students. We often find in the same classroom a boy who likes posters of puppies and kittens and a girl of the same age who is into dating, makeup, and hard rock music.

● 10s & 11s: Physical Development

These students are growing and developing at vastly different rates. Girls are often taller than boys. Growth spurts result in awkwardness and fatigue, and hormonal changes affect emotions. And, of course, kids are extremely sensitive about their differences.

Be careful about assuming that a child is either too old or too young for your classroom, because kids of this age come in all shapes and sizes. Within your lessons, make it a point to include activities that might seem too old or too young for your kids, because they have such varied interests and levels of personal security. Some kids still want to be kids while others are trying to be adults.

Kids in this age group are full of energy, but they tire easily. While they're ready for a wide variety of new experiences, they do require more rest and sleep than they did a year or two earlier. When kids participate in strenuous physical activity—at camp, for instance— they must be given sufficient (and enforced!) quiet time to rest and recover. Otherwise, poor behavior is inevitable. Overly tired kids are unable to control their emotions, their tongues, and their attitudes.

Many of these children have well-developed muscle control, yet they experience clumsiness due to dramatic growth spurts. Suddenly, feet are bigger than ever before and they just get in the way! These kids feel a great deal of personal satisfaction from mastering new skills, but they can be devastated when they feel awkward in front of their peers. Offer physical activities that challenge kids, but not to the point of risking personal humiliation.

● 10s & 11s: Intellectual Development

One thing that teachers love about these kids is their monumental curiosity. Allow time for them to explore their environment and engage in individual learning activities. Use your knowledge of their interests to engage them in the lesson. Kids who are interested stay on task!

Because fifth- and sixth-graders are so interested in everything, they can be easily distracted. Lessons need to be well-prepared, and all activities need to have a clear connection to the lesson focus. Otherwise, teachers will find themselves pulled off course.

Don't be alarmed to see kids of this age daydreaming. It's normal and to be expected. Don't get frustrated or attempt to punish kids for "checking out." Our role as teachers is to snag their attention, help them refocus, and use subtle prompts and cues to keep them on task.

Ten- and eleven-year-olds have little or no concept of time. You will need to repeatedly remind them of deadlines to register for upcoming events. Don't be surprised when they wait until the last minute (and beyond!) to sign up. You'll need to send publicity to both students and parents; otherwise, parents may never hear about the special events you've planned.

"Transescents" are interested in the real and practical. Make sure that what you are teaching is relevant to their lives and practical in its application—otherwise these kids will simply blow it off. Encourage lively discussion of how what they've just learned will affect their lives in the coming week. This kind of interaction helps us keep in touch with the lives and interests of our students. As we talk, we're able to help students see how the Bible impacts their world.

During these years, kids are making the transition from concrete thinking to abstract. You'll need to be prepared for both kinds of learners within your programs. Help kids through this transition by using open-ended questions that allow for many different responses on varying cognitive levels.

● 10s & 11s: Emotional Development

Due to hormonal changes, these kids experience frequent mood changes and may swing out of control emotionally without much apparent provocation. They jump moment by moment between love, hate, happiness, and fear. As teachers, we need to remain calm and model mature responses. It's good to remind ourselves that the child's sudden outburst has little or nothing to do with anything we've done or said. This is the time to develop "alligator hide" and let those mood swings bounce off, rather than taking them personally. Challenging or punishing kids who are being "hormonal" will only lead to more severe discipline problems.

Anger will often emerge in these kids as a result of fatigue, feelings of inadequacy, rejection, and uncertainty. Teachers need to be encouragers who frequently affirm with verbal praise, personal valuing, and appropriate physical affection. Forgiveness needs to characterize the relationship between teacher and student.

You'll find that fear tends to manifest itself in the form of worry.

Kids worry about nonacceptance, report cards, peer criticism, the increasing demands on them, and being alone in the dark. Parents and other adults will often discount these fears, saying that kids should have grown out of them by now. Nevertheless, these fears are real. The child doesn't want a baby sitter but demands a night light.

We need to be accepting and understanding of these students and recognize that no emotion is sin as long as it is acted upon in an appropriate way.

● 10s & 11s: Social Development

It's normal for a ten- or eleven-year-old to have a very close friend of the same gender. This "buddy" relationship is an essential prerequisite for later development of healthy relationships with the opposite sex. Our programs should be designed to meet this need by allowing students of the same sex to spend time together in various settings. Staff members should also model healthy relationships with other staff members of the same sex.

A variety of discipline problems can arise depending on how you group boys and girls at this age. A group of all boys will often misbehave by being rambunctious and rude, and a group of girls by themselves can be "cliquish," gossipy, and catty; but most groups will respond to a teacher's encouragement to stay on task.

Mixing sexes at this age will often result in complaints from the boys in particular, but we find that both sexes do well when you have the right group dynamics. You must have more than one or two of each sex in the group (especially with boys). Working with mixed groups gives us an opportunity to teach kids how to properly deal with the opposite sex and how to use good manners in mixed company.

We believe that both single-gender and mixed-gender activities and groupings are valuable to preadolescents. It's also helpful to have leaders of both sexes who are able to interact positively with kids in both settings. Many of these kids are children of divorce and are in need of healthy role models of both sexes.

At this vulnerable age, students become especially preoccupied with themselves and think that everyone else must be focused on them too. Just entering a room can be traumatic, because the child assumes that everyone is looking at him or her. You can help ease kids through some of these difficulties by being in the classroom early to greet kids, chat with them, and help them begin conversing with others. Keep your eye out for loners and less-popular kids who lack social skills. You might enlist the help of a sympathetic child who is comfortable playing the role of "buddy" to make others feel welcome and accepted.

This is a great time to get kids involved in service projects.

There's no better way to help them break away from their self-absorption, think about others, and realize that they can make a difference in God's world.

● 10s & 11s: Spiritual Development

Spiritually, you may find many new or renewed commitments to God and the church during these years as kids deepen their understanding of what it means to be a follower of Christ. The abstract thinker can appreciate spiritual issues in a much more personal way than the concrete child who accepts faith primarily because of his or her parents' beliefs.

The church becomes an incredibly important place for families with kids in fifth and sixth grade. God has wired these kids to enter a "leaving" stage of development. We like to think of preadolescents as two-year-olds with hormones! They want to distance themselves from their parents and seek out their own values and beliefs more than ever before. They are, however, drawn to other mature adults who can provide the guidance they still need and want—adults who are a lot like Mom and Dad. Teachers and church workers need to fill a crucial role in helping these kids in their growing relationships with God.

Peer-group influence becomes stronger as kids move toward adolescence. Because social relationships are extremely important, you will be fighting a lost cause if you try to keep these kids from talking with each other! Recognize the urge to interact and converse as a legitimate need in your students' lives. Provide for this need in a Christian context by allowing socializing during snack times, before and after class, and at regular friendship-building events. Your teaching style must also include numerous opportunities for students' interaction. Because their developing value systems are influenced by their peers, it's imperative that we include guided discussion as a key tool for exploring, understanding, and applying Bible truths.

Meeting the Needs of All Kids

No matter what the age level, kids will be kids. And when kids are bored, angry, or frustrated, they act out. Our goal as caring teachers must be to structure our lessons and classroom environment in ways that will optimize kids' abilities and eliminate distractions. And whether it's been a great day or a disaster, we want every child to feel our unconditional love.

The best way to prevent discipline problems is to make our lessons and classroom activities relevant and compelling. When children find meaning and purpose in the Christian education process, they will behave better.

3 Discipline to the Design of the Child

ur job, as teachers in the church, is to "train a child in the way he [or she] should go" (Proverbs 22:6, NIV). Our goal is in the second part of the proverb: "when he is old, he will not turn from it." In more definitive terms, the proverb means that we want to train children to be godly and moral *disciples* (learners) who have the tools, discipline, and maturity to consistently make right decisions on their own. That's quite a task. Discipline needs to be an *ongoing training process.*

We'll have the most success in completing our task when we teach, train, and discipline according to the makeup of the child. Because each child is different in personality and motivation, we must adapt our methods of training in order to engage the child's interest, cultivating in him or her a passion to know and obey God.

This chapter will help you understand how children differ from each other. Please don't forget that these differences weren't designed by God simply for the sake of variety. Each child is completely unique and gifted by God for his purposes. With limitless creativity, God crafted each child with a special blend of characteristics that makes him or her precious and necessary to God. Consider the psalmist's wonder at God's creative genius:

> *I praise you because you made me in an amazing and wonderful way. What you have done is wonderful. I know this very well. You saw my bones being formed as I took shape in my mother's body. When I was put together there, you saw my body as it was formed. All the days planned for me were written in your book before I was one day old (Psalm 139:14-16).*

God is a God of infinite variety. In a garden, some flowers bloom in the fall, some bloom in the spring, some need lots of sun, others do not, and so it goes. It's the same with children: They are unique individuals with their own distinctive needs. As teachers, we need to respond to the nature of the child God created. To maximize the potential God has placed in that child, we must be flexible in our discipline process.

Does that mean that our discipline is inconsistent? No! No matter which child we're working with, the principles remain the same because they are based on Scripture. We continue to teach biblical ethics that are solid and foundational. But as we administer discipline, we must tailor our approach to account for each child's unique characteristics. When we do that lovingly and consistently, our discipline shapes children's lives far beyond the classroom walls—it becomes instruction in righteousness.

The Whole Child

As we seek to better understand this child we are discipling, we want to move from the parts to the whole. The distinctive aspects of children that we will look at include: personality and temperament types, modalities (perceptual strengths), learning styles, preferences in environment, and multiple intelligences.

Each of these aspects of the child's God-given nature adds a key dimension to who the child is. You might think of the aspects as layers of an onion. Each part wraps itself around the others, forming the whole onion. Let's "peel back" each of these traits to take a closer look at how each part contributes to the whole child.

As you read through these descriptions, you'll discover yourself thinking of how perfectly they fit various children in your class. But keep an eye out for yourself, too! The traits that you bring to the classroom have a huge impact on your teaching style as well as the way you relate to the children in your class.

I. Personality Type and Discipline

A child's temperament is a God-given behavioral predisposition that's present at birth. As this temperament combines with life experiences and training, the personality emerges.

Each child and adult is a unique combination of these personality-temperament types. As we study the facets of personality that make each of us unique, we can identify patterns that will help us better see and understand ourselves and our students.

God imprints each of us with a pattern especially designed for his purpose. I believe that we each have one strong, dominant temperament and a weaker, secondary one. Let me share from my own personal experience. I am aware that I have two different sides to my personality. Part of me is outgoing and loves people and activity. The other part of me is very quiet and reflective and needs lots of "alone time" that enables me to go back and love the people and activity again. If I don't get alone time I feel like a porcupine with its quills out to protect

The Whole Child

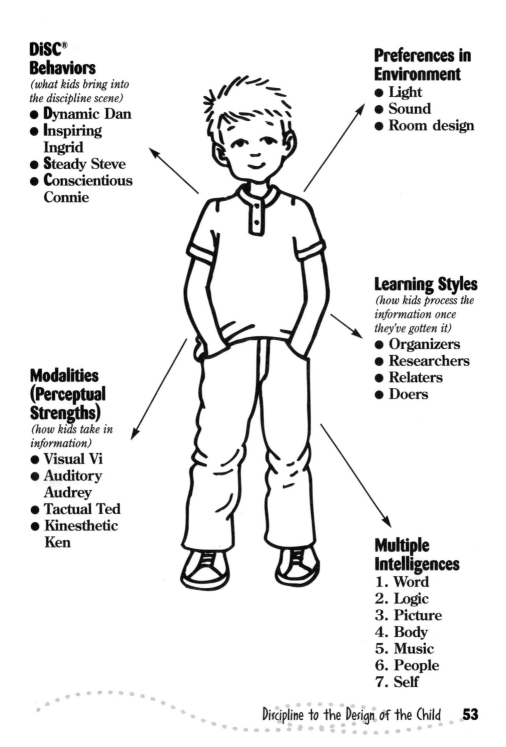

DiSC®
Behaviors
(what kids bring into
the discipline scene)
- **D**ynamic Dan
- **I**nspiring
  Ingrid
- **S**teady Steve
- **C**onscientious
  Connie

Preferences in
Environment
- Light
- Sound
- Room design

Learning Styles
(how kids process the
information once
they've gotten it)
- Organizers
- Researchers
- Relaters
- Doers

Modalities
(Perceptual
Strengths)
(how kids take in
information)
- Visual Vi
- Auditory
  Audrey
- Tactual Ted
- Kinesthetic
  Ken

Multiple
Intelligences
1. Word
2. Logic
3. Picture
4. Body
5. Music
6. People
7. Self

itself, and I find myself inwardly screaming, "Leave me alone!"

I also believe that when we become members of God's family, we will develop more balanced blends of temperaments as we allow God to work in our lives. We must remember, however, that we tend to see life through the grids of our own individual temperaments. We assume that we are "right" because this is how God made us. As teachers, we need to lovingly respect and do our best to understand children of all temperaments.

The DiSC® Model

For the purposes of this book, we have chosen the DiSC model* to describe different behaviors. The DiSC model was originally developed by Dr. William Moulton Marston. Carlson Learning Company adopted the DiSC model into a learning instrument called the Personal Profile System® which helps adults or young people better understand themselves and others.

The DiSC model gives us valuable information about key behaviors. It helps us gain a quick grasp of how our behavioral preferences compare to those of our students. From that understanding, we can predict how best to deal with students in discipline situations.

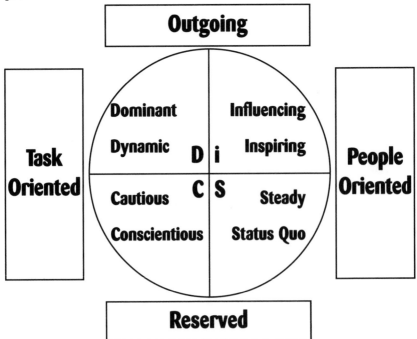

*Information about the DiSC® model and DiSC® Dimensions of Behavior is taken from the *Personal Profile System* © Copyright 1994 Carlson Learning Company, the *Biblical Personal Profile System* © Copyright 1995 Carlson Learning Company, and the *Biblical Personal Profile System* Facilitator's Guide © Copyright 1995 Carlson Learning Company, and is used with permission of Carlson Learning Company. DiSC, Personal Profile System, and Biblical Personal Profile System are registered trademarks of Carlson Learning Company, Minneapolis, Minnesota. For information call 800-777-9897.

Two of the behavioral preferences are more **people**-oriented, and two are more **task**-oriented. Depending upon where your primary behaviors fall on the chart, certain characteristics may be intensified. For example, the I (Inspiring) and the S (Steady) are both on the **people** side of the circle. Even though one of the strengths is reserved and the other is outgoing, both are people-oriented.

On the other hand, the D (Dominant) and C (Conscientious) are both on the **task** side of the circle; therefore, people with these strengths may not possess as many people skills.

Let's take a closer look at the characteristics of each of the four kinds of behaviors from the DiSC® model. We've given each either a male or female nickname simply for the sake of discussion, but people of both genders can fall into any of the four categories. We'll discover what qualities will emerge from kids who match these strengths and how we can interact with these kids in our classrooms to bring out the best in each child.

Dynamic Dan

Dynamic Dan is outgoing. He is task-oriented. Accomplishing his goals means everything to him. He wants it his way. The way to win with this child is to, first and foremost, recognize his God-given leadership ability. This child **will** be in charge of something in his lifetime, we just want to be sure it's on the Lord's team!

The more we give this child to be **in charge of,** such as selecting his clothes and organizing his room or area of the classroom, the

Dominant, **D**ynamic

- *Outgoing*
- *Task-oriented*
- *Takes authority and control*
- *Accepts challenges well*
- *Likes frequent change*
- *Active*
- *Competitive*
- *Strong-willed*
- *May challenge authority*

more positively he responds. But if you say, "Go clean up your area," what do you hear from this child? An argument! He'll give you all the reasons in the world why he shouldn't have to do it. This kid can talk his way out of anything. He wants control.

So we hand him control by saying, "Dan, you may be in charge of cleaning your area (or room) today." When he hears that you're offering him an opportunity to be in charge, he's more willing to cooperate.

Remember, with this child it's all in how you package it. If he thinks he is in control and can do things on his terms, he's fine. For him, powering through the task at hand is everything.

Words that work well for this child are: "I wonder if you can do it faster than you did last week, Dan?" Because he's so competitive, you may get this kind of response: "I'm gonna do it faster this week. You time me, OK?"

For Dan, guidelines work better than rules. And he appreciates being allowed to make choices. "Dan, you may clean up your area and then get your Bible or you may get your Bible and then clean up your area." You give him options within the boundaries of what's acceptable to you, but because he gets to choose, he still feels he has some aspect of "control" in the situation.

With this child, you must discipline with strength to match his need to control every step of the way. But you'll have more success if you affirm his strength rather than fighting it. If that's outside your personality comfort-zone, it may be difficult.

What happens when you're a laid-back, easygoing parent or teacher and you've got one of these kids? Because this child must "win," you need to give him lots of opportunities to win in an appropriate way. We want to develop the godly leadership ability in this child, and that begins by encouraging a listening spirit and a willingness to serve.

Dynamic Dan wants control, so we discipline by giving choices that fall within the parameters of desired behavior; making choices allows him to be "in charge."

James scored high in the D quadrant and was known by all as "*The Discipline Problem.*" He was your basic "high D" child: very dynamic, demanding, and driving! His new, well-meaning teacher in the third-grade class decided to confront James on the very first Sunday, hoping to ward off future problems. She stated, "James, I have heard about you, and I just want you to know, you *will* obey me." Oops! James, your basic strong-willed child, responded as any high D child will—with complete defiance. The teacher responded with a will to match James' intense will, and the battle lines were drawn.

The worse James got, the more controlling the teacher became. Everyone was losing. With this fierce battle going on every Sunday, the teacher was tense and James grew more belligerent. But the other children in the class were the biggest losers. The focus in the classroom was not on teaching the Word of God, but on determining who was going to "win" that Sunday. Finally, the teacher sent James to the office.

The children's director asked God to help her see James from

God's perspective—what she saw was a leader in the making. She affirmed James' God-given gifts as a leader. She talked with him to help him understand what being God's leader was all about, telling him that leadership begins with a submissive spirit and a servant heart. She began to help him understand why obeying those in authority was important. She prayed with him. She invited him to use his leadership gifts to help her. James began to turn around.

High D children are strong, and they can outlast most adults. Trying to "out-control" one of these children usually exhausts the teacher and exhilarates the child!

What's the solution? Build a positive, trusting relationship with the child; show her that you believe in her; and help him use his God-given gifts in a positive way.

Inspiring Ingrid

Inspiring Ingrid is outgoing. She is a fun-loving child. She is a joy to have in the classroom and at home, but she may be a little talkative and forgetful. She gets "rule amnesia" and needs to be reminded often of your expectations.

nspiring, nfluencing

- *Outgoing*
- *Entertaining*
- *Loves to help*
- *Spontaneous*
- *Talkative*
- *Loves people*
- *Forgetful at times*
- *Volunteers often*
- *Popular*
- *Optimistic*

Inspiring Ingrid wants to have fun, so you discipline with humor and with games. Words that work well for this child are "I wonder if…" For example, you might say, "I wonder if we could get our room cleaned up so fast that we would have time to play a game."

Inspiring Ingrid is not intrinsically motivated to clean! When the classroom is trashed and you say, "Cleanup time," Inspiring Ingrid does not say, "Cool! I'll help!" She doesn't even see the need to take care of the mess.

Perhaps you've even given a little unsolicited advice such as, "Be sure to put the books in the bookcase and the games in the closet." After a few minutes, you'll notice that Ingrid is missing. Where do you find her? In the closet, with 29 zillion game pieces spread on the floor around her! You say, "I told you to put the games away." She says, "But Teacher, I found all these neat games in here that I haven't played in a long time—this is fun!"

In response, you don't say, "You just forgot; it's all right." But you understand that an Inspiring Ingrid is likely to forget. She gets rule amnesia. A good strategy is to make the cleanup job into a game.

For example, this is a game I used to play with my child Angela when I wanted her to clean her room. I'd say something like, "Angela, I'm really sorry, honey, but you are not going to be able to go up to your room for a couple of days."

"Why not, Mom?"

"Well, honey, there's that red tape across the door that you may have noticed. The government was here, and they declared your room a federal disaster area (heavy, exaggerated sigh). When I've got an extra three or four days, I'll be glad to help you dig that room out, OK?"

Then she probably would say, "OK, Mommy," and continue to play. Now, I know my daughter, and she likes to play games with me, too. She might "sneak" out the front door and quietly come in the back door. I may hear little steps, but I just pretend that I don't know she's there.

Then she'll tiptoe out the back door, come in the front door, and say, "Mommy, would you have a little time to help me at least get started?"

And I'd say, "Oh, I guess so, but it's going to take a really long time..." When we get to her room...Surprise! It's clean! (Please understand that I use the term "clean" loosely.)

The point is, saying to this child, "Go clean your room right now!" just won't work. But when you make it into a game, you're far more likely to get positive results. Your entertaining Inspiring Ingrid responds well when you:

✓ use humor,

✓ make it into a game, and

✓ use the words "I wonder if..."

Steady, Shy, Status Quo

- *Reserved*
- *People-oriented*
- *Patient*
- *Peacemaker*
- *Observer*
- *Easygoing*
- *Calm*
- *Compliant*
- *Quiet*
- *Keeps emotions hidden, may withdraw*

Steady Steve

Steady Steve is reserved. He is a peacemaker and a compliant child. He makes you look really good as a parent or teacher because he actually obeys you! If you say, "We don't touch that," he doesn't need to touch it—unlike the high D child who will look you straight in the eye and touch it!

It's easy to forget Steady Steve because he's so quiet and easygoing. However, this is the child who may make a joke behind your back. He has a quiet kind of wit, and because he has such good interior organization, he can make a joke on the periphery and watch the whole class "lose it" while he remains seemingly stoic.

The S child is sooooo easy to discipline, or so it seems! Yes, he can appear so compliant, so innocent—but I have learned over the years that this child may "getcha" from time to time. I have also learned that this child will usually operate behind your back because of his reserved nature.

One Sunday when I was putting something on the board, I heard the dreaded, infamous ripple of quiet laughter. I knew that my Steady Steve had been at work, so, with a smile on my face, I asked him what he had said.

"Well, ma'am, " he responded, "I said your bra fell off."

I fought back a giggle and responded in a most professional manner, "Thank you for that information, Stephen, but I believe that I would know if that happened."

Of course, the whole class was chuckling as he answered, "No, ma'am, it really did. Look." I turned to look at the board.

Now, gentlemen, just skip this story because you will never understand. But ladies, do you remember when we used to buy the removable foam shoulder-pads that came in a little can with the deceptive advertising that said **"Will Stay on Your Shoulders"** printed boldly on the label? Now, I ask you, did they **ever** stay on? No! They roamed.

Well, there at the board was the traveling shoulder-pad! As I was writing, my foam shoulder-pad took on a will of its own and made its way to the floor. To Stephen's untrained eye, it appeared to be a more intimate piece of apparel!

That is the S child; ever-quiet, seemingly ever-innocent, but beware!

If you want to see the "back side" of this child, push him. He does not respond well to being pushed—that's when you'll see stubbornness emerge. But if you give him the time he needs to complete tasks and warn him when that time is nearly up, he responds well. Words that work well with this child are, "Steve, you need to get your area cleaned up in five minutes."

Steady Steve is a peacemaker, so he responds well when you:

✓ enjoy his humor (without letting him become disrespectful), and

✓ give him acceptable limits for completing a task.

For example, to an older S child you might say, "Steve, you have until ten o'clock to get the art materials put away. You may put them away whenever you want as long as you get it done by ten."

This is effective because he likes operating on his own timetable.

With a younger S child, you might say, "In five minutes we'll begin to clean up our toys…In three minutes we'll begin to clean up our toys…Now it's time to clean up our toys."

Remember, S children can seem easygoing and compliant, but in reality they may be "stuffing" their emotions and moving toward a passive-rebellious mind-set. We want to stay close in touch with these kids to make sure these habits don't begin.

Conscientious, Contemplative

- Reserved
- Task-oriented
- Very sensitive to other people
- Complies with authority
- Enjoys routine and loves schedules
- Very conscientious
- Overly perfectionistic
- Idealistic
- Thinks things through
- Compassionate

Conscientious Connie

Conscientious Connie is reserved. Connie is very sensitive. Games do not work with this child. If you try disciplining with a game, it will bomb. She can't tell when you're playing a game because to her, everything is serious.

This is a grown-up in a child's body. And please, for goodness sake, don't say, "Lighten up, Connie, these are the best years of your life." For starters, she can't lighten up. Secondly, childhood is not her finest hour, and if you tell her this is the best, she will think as she plummets into deep despair, "This is as good as it gets!?!??!?!?!"

What this child needs from you is hope. When she is discouraged, you can tell her, "You'll be much happier as an adult. We simply have to get you through this time called childhood."

Conscientious Connie needs to do it "right." So with this child, you discipline with sensitivity and predictability. She gets very unnerved if things aren't happening in order. In her mind she sees the ideal and perfection, but we live in a fallen, sinful world where everything and everyone falls short. She gets "paralysis of analysis" when things don't go quite the way she thinks they should or if she is overwhelmed by a task.

We need to remember that Connie is a die-hard perfectionist. Nothing less than the best will do. So when you give her a task, you must first set up a system so she'll know how to begin.

Let's use an example from home. You've just told Connie to clean her room. You go to her room, and she is standing in the middle of the room, catatonic. She is in dire misery and would love to reflect this misery back to you because you're the one who made her feel this way. In fact, she may lash out at you because, after all, you are the cause of all this pain. Just realize that she is stuck emotionally and that you need to help her get unstuck.

You could begin by saying, "Connie, make your bed. When your bed is made, tell me and I will come back to check." Then you give her another task: "Now, let's put away your clothes." You continue in this manner by breaking the job down into measurable tasks.

You might make a diagram of the overall task by writing the steps around the edge of a clock face with the first task positioned by one o'clock. Place a photograph of the cleaned room at twelve o'clock. Place the diagram on the wall near the light switch so Connie can refer to it again and again. You can adapt this chart to suit any classroom situation. Just remember that your goal is to help the C child get over her fear of imperfection and get started on the task at hand.

Conscientious Connie isn't the type to deliberately defy you—she simply gets emotionally stuck if she thinks she can't do something perfectly. This child requires an enormous amount of encouragement.

C children are often unable to be spontaneous because rules and standards are so important to them.

A mother had told her children that they would go to the library after school. It had been raining for a week, but in the early afternoon, the sun suddenly came out and it turned into a gorgeous day. When the mother picked up her children from school, she said: "Surprise! We're going to the park because it's such a beautiful day!"

The I (inspiring, influencing) child had "forgotten" the previous plan and promptly yelled, "Great!"

The C child looked pensively at the mother and finally said, "But Mom, you said we were going to the library," to which the mother replied, "Yes, but look what a great day it is!"

The C child continued, "But Mom, you lied. You **said** we were going to the library..."

The bottom line with this child is that if we say we're going to do something, we'd better deliver! This child will hold our feet to the fire and make us keep our commitments. To be comfortable, the C child must have consistency.

Conscientious Connie is a very sensitive child who wants to do it **right,** so we discipline with:

✓ predictability,

✓ sensitivity, and

✓ tons of encouragement.

II. Discipline to the Modality of the Child

All children are multisensory learners. They learn best when they can see something, hear it, touch it, and with little ones, taste it and sometimes smell it. But each child tends to favor one sense as a tool for learning. We use the term learning modality to describe the sense that best enables each of us to take in information.

The four main learning modalities for children are:

1. **Visual modality:** *see it*
2. **Auditory modality:** *hear it*
3. **Tactual modality:** *touch it*
4. **Kinesthetic modality:** *do it*

Many of our Christian education programs do not teach in the way that children learn best. Much of what happens in traditional Sunday school classes is designed for visual learners—children who learn best by seeing something. These children are usually good readers, can quickly grasp things that they see, and like work sheets. But visual learners account for only one-third of all children.

What about the other two-thirds? A smaller percentage of them are auditory learners, which means that they need to hear information and talk about it in order to assimilate it. Talking usually goes on in the teaching process, and these children can grasp the subject at that time. But when they go back to their places for "seatwork," suddenly it is all Greek to them! It is vital that a teacher or parent patiently explains the subject matter to them again and allows them to verbalize what they are learning.

That leaves us with almost one-half of all children who need to touch something in order to understand it. They simply cannot learn as well with just visual or auditory input. They have to touch, but there is nothing to touch except a book, a pencil, or a work sheet, and frankly, those don't count as kinesthetic learning tools. In a typical classroom or Sunday school, these kids (nearly one half of all children) won't do as well as they could in a more active learning environment.

While traditional teaching methods work well with some students (visual and auditory learners), these methods often turn off other kids (tactual and kinesthetic learners). We need to adapt our teaching methods to meet the needs of all children. To better understand the differences in the four learning modalities, let's take a tour of the four main modalities by meeting four imaginary kids.

Visual Vi

Visual Vi has her eye out for information. She needs to see it. This child works well with charts that allow her to track her projects visually by checking things off or adding stars or stickers. So discipline with visuals. Visual Vi is always watching your body language. When you've about had it, she can see it in your eyes. The wise teacher makes it a point to "speak" to Vi with body language.

Visual

- *Learn best when they can see it.*
- *Generally like reading and are comfortable with the written word.*
- *Like to write things down.*
- *Like charts and graphs.*
- *Like working in workbooks and on work sheets.*
- *Usually prefer a quiet working environment.*
- *Generally prefer their working environment to be orderly before they begin.*

Visual Vi needs to *see it,* so we discipline by:

✓ posting the rules,

✓ making eye contact, and

✓ using charts to check off behavior and tasks accomplished.

These are the kinds of comments you might hear from visual learners:

✓ "If I could see it, I would remember it."

✓ "I see what you mean."

✓ "If I write it down, I will remember it better."

Auditory Audrey

Auditory Audrey needs to hear and talk about new information, so you discipline by having her repeat what you've told her. If this child consistently fails to follow instructions, just say "Audrey, what did I tell you to do?" and let her verbalize it. All she needs is that auditory feedback.

When we realize that a lot of the blurting out and excessive talking are factors relating to a learning style rather than to a discipline problem, we can be more sensitive in correcting an auditory child. That doesn't mean we let this child interrupt or dominate the classroom,

Auditory

- *Learn best when they interact verbally.*
- *Like to be read to or to read out loud rather than reading silently. They often move their lips when they're reading silently.*
- *Like to listen to tapes and CDs. They can more easily remember things that are set to music.*
- *Generally work better with background music or other sounds.*
- *Like panels, debates, and storytelling.*
- *Generally are not bothered by disorder in the environment.*
- *Ask a lot of questions for better understanding. They can be misunderstood as not paying attention.*
- *Don't like written work and reading and therefore are considered to not be applying themselves.*

but we remember that when we can give her a chance to verbalize, she will be easier to deal with. When this child is so anxious to speak that she's about to go into orbit, just say, "Audrey, I'm going to give you a chance to talk; you just have to wait a minute."

John was an auditory learner who would talk whether someone else was in the room or not! Any time he made eye contact with an adult, he would begin with "Did you know…?" He rarely knew what he was going to say, he only knew that he wanted to talk. He would often get into trouble for blurting out information that rarely related to the teacher's topic. The class would follow his train of thought, such as it was, and the teacher would get very frustrated. The more she tried to get John to stay quiet, the more he seemed to want to talk.

As the teacher began to understand John's talking as a need for auditory closure, she began to make progress with him. Instead of getting angry, she trained him to raise his hand and then wait to be called on. When she could see that he was practically hyperventilating in his desire to speak, she would smile and say: "I know you need to talk, John. Just wait a minute and I will call on you." This helped to build up his ability to wait to speak rather than blurting things out impulsively.

The teacher encouraged his parents to try this "game" at home. When John wanted to speak, he would approach his parents. If they were talking to each other or to someone else, John would put his hand on one of their shoulders. When they looked at him, he could ask for permission to speak.

Auditory Audrey needs to *hear information and talk about it,* so we discipline by:

✓ having her repeat information back to us,

✓ using lots of voice inflection, and

✓ always remembering to lower our voices at the end of a sentence, especially a disciplinary sentence. Something to remember: When we (especially women) get upset, our voices go up in pitch and in decibel level and then children may not take us seriously.

Tactual Ted

Tactual Ted likes to touch. He is generally not a motor-driven (hyperactive) child, he simply needs to touch. If his hands don't have something constructive to do, he will find something mischievous to do!

Tactual children doodle on their papers (and get marked down a letter grade), make their papers into fleets of airplanes, or play with the hair of the little girl in front of them.

If a child is extremely tactual, I am not opposed to letting him or her have a squeeze ball to "smoosh" as long as it stays in a pocket.

Tactual

- *Learn best when they can touch things.*
- *Like to "fiddle" with things.*
- *Like to take things apart to see how they work.*
- *Generally are not as "motor-driven" (hyperactive) as kinesthetic children.*
- *Comprehend more quickly when using manipulatives.*
- *Learn best by doing.*
- *Need hands-on experiences.*
- *Need to be taught adaptive skills, such as taking notes and highlighting.*

But here's an important rule of thumb: *When I let children have special privileges that suit their learning styles, I say: "This is a tool to help you, not a toy. If you abuse it, you lose it."*

When teachers are talking, they generally feel more secure when all the children are looking right at them with their little hands folded in their laps. This gives the false illusion that all the children are listening and that their little precious lives are being transformed by this life-changing lesson.

The truth is that some children can listen better when their little hands are busy! These children are the tactual learners. Their hands need to move in order for them to learn most effectively. My years of experience have taught me to trust how God has divinely wired his children. Instead of making children sit like perfect little robots, I show them trust by letting them do something that helps them learn. The only rule is that they not disturb others! So I let children doodle as I teach if it helps them learn more effectively.

Obviously, the best teaching is active learning when the children are involved. But there are times when children need to be quiet and listen. If children need to draw or doodle during these times, it should be allowed.

Tactual learners need to *touch,* so we accommodate them by:

✓ involving them in hands-on activities,

✓ allowing discreet use of squeeze balls or doodle pads, and

✓ reminding them that manipulatives must not distract others.

Kinesthetic

● *Learn best when their bodies are in motion.*
● *Learn best by doing.*
● *Need a hands-on, multisensory approach.*
● *Are "motor-driven."*
● *May have A.D.D. (Attention Deficit Disorder), but many do not. Investigate before you medicate!*
● *Do not do well under bright fluorescent light.*
● *Need to memorize with some corresponding body movement such as sign language.*

Kinesthetic Ken

Kinesthetic Ken needs to move, so you discipline by giving him lots of chances to move. He responds best to an active-learning approach. With this child, we have to take time to direct and redirect.

You might ask, "Ken, what task are you doing right now?" Or you might give Ken a "secret" signal you've worked out in advance, such as touching your earlobe or crossing your fingers.

Many of Kinesthetic Ken's classroom problems stem from the fact that in some situations, his body moves faster than his brain. Recognize that a lot of what you see from him is not necessarily deliberate disobedience. Always look this child in the eyes. If you see rebellion in his eyes, deal with that. Discipline the rebellion, but don't discipline every little movement because the movement may just be his learning style.

If you send these children to the time-out chair every time they move, they will spend the best years of their lives in the time-out chair. Envision this Sunday afternoon conversation between Kinesthetic Ken and his parents.

"What did you do in Sunday school today?"

"I sat in the time-out chair."

"What did you learn?"

"Sit down. Sit down. Be still."

That is not the message we want our children to take home from

Sunday school, is it?

Kinesthetic Ken needs full-body movement in order to learn best, so we discipline by:

✓ directing and redirecting,

✓ utilizing meaningful eye contact, and

✓ providing hands-on learning that allows him to do something as he learns new concepts.

The Kinesthetic Continuum

This continuum illustrates a key concept about children's activity levels. It's important to understand this, because there are currently so many misconceptions about A.D.D. and hyperactivity.

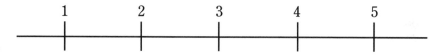

The first point on the continuum is the **normal** amount of movement that each of us needs to do. The second point is **tactual,** and that is for the person who needs to touch. The third point is to designate the **kinesthetic** learner. This is the person who needs full-body movement in order to learn. The fourth point designates A.D.D. which is Attention Deficit Disorder without the hyperactive component. The fifth point designates A.D.H.D. which is A.D.D. with the hyperactive component.

This is the important point to remember. Children who have A.D.D. are usually tactual as their primary learning modality. Children who have A.D.H.D. are usually kinesthetic as their primary learning modality. But not every child who is tactual or kinesthetic has A.D.D. or A.D.H.D. (There will be more on this point in Chapter 5.) At the very heart of this misunderstanding lies the bulk of the misdiagnosis of A.D.D.

Seasons of Learning

All truth is God's truth. This becomes particularly evident when we relate old learning models to contemporary research. The *Trivium,* an educational model that dates back to the Middle Ages, states that there are three seasons of learning: the Grammar Stage, the Dialectic Stage, and the Rhetoric Stage. It's critically important for teachers in the church to recognize and respect what goes on in kids' minds as they pass through each of these seasons of learning.

● **The Grammar Stage** is roughly equivalent to the time children spend in elementary school. In fact, this stage is the basis for the old-fashioned term "grammar school." During these years, children learn the language of a subject. They learn the languages of phonics, of math and numbers, and of spelling rules. This is the age when children love to learn Bible stories.

It's not hard to detect when kids are ready to graduate to the next level—we've all gotten "the look" from a child in the junior department. This look is a challenge that says, "I dare you to teach me something I don't already know!" It announces that a child has moved into the Dialectic Stage.

● **The Dialectic Stage** is when children need to Debate, Dispute, and enter into Dialogue about everything we've taught them in the Grammar Stage. If we observe students as they leave the junior department and move on to middle school or junior high, we have to notice their intensity on the auditory level (which, being interpreted, means—they're **loud!**). Regardless of a child's main learning modality, they *all* begin to be very auditory beginning between the ages of eleven to thirteen and continuing until about age fifteen.

Please understand that it is developmentally appropriate for kids to become loud. We blame all of their "ill behavior" on hormones, but I am convinced that much of this behavior is kids' intrinsic need to be auditory as well as very disputatious (which, being interpreted, means—leaning slightly to the ornery side of argumentative).

One of the first signs that a child has entered the Dialectic Stage is the appendage which grows from the ear, otherwise known as the telephone. Besides the telephone, there's something else kids have to have or "die," and that something is music. Ah, here we see kids entering into what is technically known in intellectual circles as "La-La Land." This behavior which can be so annoying to adults is both normal and, I believe, God–ordained. Why?

> We need teachers in this critically important stage
> who will *love* and *accept* these kids. Effective
> teachers feel *comfortable* allowing kids to question
> various aspects of the Christian faith.

This dialectic time is the season in which our children take ownership of their faith. It is both *necessary* and *proper* for kids to take what we have given them in the Grammar Stage and argue it to death in the Dialectic Stage. If we can love and guide them through this time, they will learn to internalize, articulate, and defend their faith. Children who are allowed to work through this process will embrace their faith and will not walk away from the church.

If we "shut them up" and blame their behavior on hormones, we cause kids to miss a most essential time in their faith development. Yes, discipline can be a challenge with kids in the Dialectic Stage. We need both wisdom and patience. This is when teachers make an *investment* in kids that can change their lives forever. If we can walk with kids down this precarious path, they *will* come out refined and able to be sincere, articulate ambassadors for Jesus Christ. They are ready for stage three, the Rhetoric Stage.

● **The Rhetoric Stage** arrives when students have grown in the Grammar Stage, have debated everything to death in the Dialectic Stage, and through that process have been empowered to communicate the Christian faith that they've woven into the very fabric of their beings. This student is prepared to deal with a society that daily reflects a world-view that is contrary and often hostile to the Christian worldview.

This stage should be the end product of all our efforts in Christian education. The world needs kids like this. And the church needs teachers who can wisely and patiently mentor kids through each season of learning.

III. Discipline to the Learning Style of the Child

After we have taken in information through our perceptual (modality) strengths, we need to **process** the information. These processes can often be seen in consistent patterns known as **learning styles.** Again, there are many systems on the market that measure and evaluate the learning-style process, and each system has developed its own names for various learning styles. For this book's purposes, we've chosen four descriptive words that sum up the primary characteristics of these four patterns.

Organizers

These children like things presented in a very logical sequence. When a teacher or a parent is disorganized, these children may "act up" because they are out of their comfort zone. They respond well to a clearly identifiable list of rules. They love structure and readily obey when things are orderly and predictable.

We can describe Organizers as learners who:
- ✓ are logical,
- ✓ are linear in thinking,
- ✓ are sequential,
- ✓ are organized, and
- ✓ thrive on predictability.

To best discipline these children, we must provide:
- ✓ structure,
- ✓ predictability,
- ✓ dependability,
- ✓ clearly stated instructions,
- ✓ advance notice,
- ✓ logical sequences, and
- ✓ consistent follow-through.

Researchers

These children always want to know the "why" for everything as well as the "how." They love facts and objective learning. For the most part, these children will not pose discipline problems unless they become discontent because they believe that you're not challenging them to think.

We can describe Researchers as learners who:
- ✓ use logic and reason;
- ✓ are intellectual;
- ✓ are analytical;
- ✓ excel in research;
- ✓ enjoy documentation;
- ✓ thrive on synthesis, theories, and models; and
- ✓ can be aloof and absent-minded.

To best discipline these children, we must provide:
- ✓ credibility;
- ✓ consistency;
- ✓ justice;
- ✓ logical consequences;
- ✓ no arbitrary rules;
- ✓ well-thought-out systems; and
- ✓ facts, not feelings.

Relaters

These are subjective children who want to know the "who" in any learning situation because they are "people." They love to relate to a subject. They pose discipline problems when there is too much objective information being presented with paper and pencil and not enough personal interaction. For these children, the secret of discipline lies in their **relationships** with the teacher.

We can describe Relaters as learners who:
- ✓ enjoy the abstract world of feelings and emotions,
- ✓ are relational,

✓ enjoy subjective exchanges,
✓ are emotional and perceptive,
✓ are imaginative and creative,
✓ think with their hearts, and
✓ have a strong need for approval.

To best discipline these children, we must provide:
✓ nurturing relationships,
✓ a sense of fairness,
✓ love that promotes self-esteem,
✓ subjective discussions about "why,"
✓ opportunities for personal interaction,
✓ approval, and
✓ generous praise and affirmation.

Doers

These children want **action!** They are your hands-on, active, "learn-from-multiple-sources" kind of children. And yes, they tend to be your classic behavior problems because they are not afraid to make their needs known. Make friends with these children outside of the discipline scene. If they think you understand and believe in them, they will respond much better in the heat of a discipline situation.

We can describe Doers as learners who:
✓ like the concrete world of activity,
✓ also enjoy the abstract world of intuition,
✓ are instinctive,
✓ tend to be impulsive,
✓ prefer to be independent,
✓ are creative and resourceful, and
✓ can think on their feet.

To best discipline these children, we must provide:
✓ guidelines rather than rules,
✓ affirmation for natural leadership abilities,
✓ opportunities to "be in charge,"
✓ choices within defined parameters, and
✓ empowerment rather than confrontation.

IV. Discipline and the Environment

Here's a little "test" for you. If you had a task to do, such as filling out a lengthy form or reading an instruction manual, where would you go to work on it? Would you sit at a desk or table in a quiet area with bright light? Or would you sit on a bed, a rocker, a recliner, or on the floor in a room with soft lighting and background sound such as music or the television?

If you work better in a quiet area with bright light and you prefer sitting at a desk, you may be more left-brain, or analytical. Analytics like bright light; they like it quiet; they like a table or a desk. So the traditional ways that most schools and churches are set up work for the analytical child. We provide bright lights, seat kids at desks or tables, and tell them to be quiet. Analytics process in a logical, linear way and respond well to the traditional learning environment. But what about the rest of the children?

If you work better sitting on a bed, a rocker, a recliner, or the floor in a room with soft light and sound, you may be more comfortable functioning out of the right side of your brain. You may be a global learner. You see the big picture quickly and then later begin to notice the details. Kinesthetic children are often global learners. They do **not** do well in the traditional learning environment. We may need to make some adaptations in the environment for our global learners. We can do much in the area of preventive discipline by allowing times for these children to work on the floor and move around.

Analytics (logical, linear thinkers) prefer:
● bright light,
● quiet, and
● working at desks or tables.

Globals (typically creative and/or kinesthetic children) prefer:
● soft light,
● soft sound, and
● freedom to move around.

How does this information factor into discipline? Many children **become** discipline problems because it's hard for them to sit still and listen for a long time. We can actually measure physiological reactions that demonstrate that global children become more restless when they are seated under a bright fluorescent light. Simply moving these children away from a bright light can help with their behavior. Many teachers will vouch for the fact that when they turn off the overhead lights and use just natural light from the window or a soft lamp, the children become less active and more peaceful.

This simple look at just three components within the environment can make classroom discipline much easier to manage. We each function out of both sides of our brain. But when we learn new information, we function out of the dominant side, and that's the side of the brain that factors into the discipline scene.

According to the research done by Dr. Rita and Dr. Kenneth Dunn from St. John's University, there are twenty-one environmental factors that affect learning. We have just looked at the three main ones: light, sound, and seating arrangement. If you would like more information, you'll find resources listed in the annotated bibliography at the end of the book.

Here's how you can apply this information in preventive discipline techniques.

Use these guidelines to structure your classroom for children who are more **global, active, and creative.**

● Seat them away from overhead fluorescent lighting.

● Allow them to move around or work on the floor rather than requiring them to sit at desks or tables in straight rows.

● Play quiet background music as they work.

● Arrange their work areas in places with minimum distractions; avoid placing them near an interactive bulletin board, a pencil sharpener, or a lively activity center.

● Take time to help these children see the big picture and then break it into component parts that they can handle without feeling overwhelmed.

● Provide a balance of structured time and informal time for movement. It's essential to provide active-learning segments during which the child can move around and participate in hands-on activities. Realize that this is a plus for both the child and the teacher because allowing for movement during the lesson addresses this child's need to be active and reduces the potential for behavior problems.

The teaching profession often attracts people who like to organize things in a logical, orderly manner. Children who need to move in order to learn often violate the comfort zone of these teachers. Strong-willed children can also drive these teachers crazy! The more we understand God's design for these children, the more effective we will be in teaching and disciplining them.

Just keep saying to yourself, "Think what these kids could do in God's kingdom with all this **energy** focused into doing the Lord's work!" This change of attitude will help you in channeling their energy positively and creatively.

Parents and teachers often become weary dealing with global, active children, and rightfully so—they can be exhausting! But, properly guided, trained, and taught, these children can do incredible things! Pray for God to give you a window to better see these children as God designed them to be!

V. Multiple Intelligences and Discipline

The classroom is a minisociety in which we need order and an environment that fosters respect for other's differences and a willingness to facilitate each other's successes. The concept of multiple intelligences helps us see that there are different ways of being "smart." When students are learning and being disciplined through their intelligence strengths, they can achieve optimum success.

The concept of multiple intelligences was developed by Dr. Howard Gardner. This concept is further developed by Dr. Thomas Armstrong in his book, *Multiple Intelligences in the Classroom.*

Here is a brief explanation of the seven different intelligences and suggested applications for the classroom. For a more in-depth look at this fascinating subject, see Armstrong's and Gardner's books listed in the annotated bibliography.

Linguistic Intelligence: Word Smart

Linguistic children like words and "self talk" and can train themselves into more positive behaviors when given a chance to use these strengths. Sarah, a child with "word smarts," responded well when I told her why we don't do a particular activity. I gave her a positive alternative plan to use when she wanted to try a negative one. We collectively came up with a short list of why we do a certain activity in a positive way and then she came up with three fun words that rhymed. She recited these rhyming words to herself when she felt tempted to try the more negative route.

Use these strategies with word-smart kids.

✓ Talk with the student.

✓ Teach the child self-talk strategies to help him or her with control issues.

✓ Use a rhyme or rap to communicate important pieces of information or patterns of behavior.

Logical Mathematical Intelligence: Logic Smart

Logical Larry was giving the teacher a hard time in class. He exasperated her; she became more emotional every time he wanted to know "why." Every time he asked, she replied **"Because I said so, that's why!"** With each repetition of this phrase, her voice became higher, until she was leaning toward the "screaming" end of the vocal spectrum. Larry continued to act up until I was asked to intervene.

Larry and I discussed the situation calmly in my office. I told him the reason for the rule, why he had to follow it, and what would happen if he chose not to follow it. He was fine after that. These children are rarely discipline problems if the rules and consequences are clearly stated.

Use these strategies with logic-smart kids.

✓ Teach them the "why" of a rule.

✓ Help them see the logic of a given behavior.

✓ Apply logical consequences.

Spatial Intelligence: Picture Smart

Picture Patty could be a discipline problem. She wasn't doing well in school. She rarely turned her homework in, and she did poorly on tests. Eventually she got sent to my office. I keep lots of games in my office that I feel represent some of the "black holes" that children come across in life. One of these black holes is long division. Long division is a visual, left-brain, logical process, and the pattern isn't easily seen by a picture-smart child when it is only presented on paper in black and white. So Patty and I did the bright, colorful long division game in my office as we talked through her behavior. As she "saw" the process of long division, she began to "see" that she was getting into trouble in school.

These children are often behavior problems because they think in pictures that are more global (right-brain) and concrete (the need to see and touch). When they are asked to process information in a structured, abstract way, their brains "don't get the picture" and they may feel stupid and inadequate. When this happens, they may channel their energy into misdeeds instead of focusing on the task at hand. Picture Patty can often draw a concept with perfect understanding, but she cannot get a good grade on an objective test. We need to empower the Picture Pattys of the world with the tools of the wonderful intelligence they possess.

Use these strategies with picture-smart kids.

✓ Since they think in pictures, help these students see the "big picture."

✓ Show videos that depict character qualities that embody what you are teaching.

✓ Use brightly colored visuals.

✓ Allow them to draw what they've learned.

Bodily Kinesthetic Intelligence: Body Smart

We sometimes hear the expression "dumb jock." This statement makes the assumption that a person who is body smart has a lower IQ than others. I, for one, am sure this is not true for I possess none of this intelligence and as a result I feel stupid many times! I truly respect people who can function well with their hands and bodies.

Once again, if we ask these children to sit still, listen, and then write out answers to questions, they will fail to reveal how smart they truly are. The movie *IQ* was a wonderful depiction of the contrast between bodily kinesthetic intelligence and logical mathematic intelligence. Guess what? Both are equally needed to make this world function! Just as each spiritual gift is important, so is each intelligence.

I was doing a teacher training at my own church. The Junior Department head was walking around in the back of the room, appearing to be helpful as latecomers straggled in. I have learned that those who volunteer for these jobs and for setting up chairs and other physical tasks tend to have bodily kinesthetic intelligence.

Now this particular man was the president of a major corporation and highly intellectual. Afterward, he seemed eager to talk. "Now I understand something for the first time in my life," he exclaimed. "When I was in training to be a Marine and we had to learn very complicated maneuvers, we would do terribly. One day, the trainer threw the book at us and said: "I don't care if you live or die, because obviously you don't. Just go out and do it, and you'll figure it out!" Guess what? They could all do it! They just couldn't sit and learn how to do it.

This is true of precious bodily kinesthetic learners. They are truly discipline problems until you let them do something.

For one year as a part of our teacher training, I told the teachers I would go in and teach any class they wanted and they could observe. My only rule: No work sheets! In fact, I state that I am allergic to work sheets!

When I went into one class, I could feel that the children were ready to explode. When I came in, the teacher said, "If I could just rubber cement their little bottoms on their chairs, I know they could get this done." What exciting task were they doing? Map skills work sheets. Yep! You would have to glue my bottom down also if you wanted me to stay on that task.

I took them outside to the garden. With our hands we made land forms. We made all the topographical areas and yes, we did get dirty. But that's why God made soap and water.

I sent a note home, asking all the children to bring clay, aluminum pans, dirt, flowers, rocks, and **whatever else they wanted** with them to class. We each created our own world, complete with lakes, bays, mountains, rivers, and volcanoes (which erupted courtesy of some of our more bodily kinesthetic boys). We worked for two hours building our projects. The teacher was most surprised to find out that no one was a discipline problem that day. Imagine that.

Bodily kinesthetic children aren't easy for many teachers to have in class, but they can be managed if we work with their need to move.

Use these strategies with body-smart kids.

✓ Use active learning.
✓ Offer creative, open-ended projects.
✓ Allow time to **do** rather than sit.

Musical Intelligence: Music Smart

Signs of this intelligence often surface sooner than signs of other intelligences. The musical child-prodigy is often identifiable by age four. In these kids, music ability seems to bubble up spontaneously, often without formal training.

Musical Mary sang while she worked. She sang in the hallways. She hummed during prayer time. She drove everyone nuts. Mary danced her way to my office. Hmm…what to do? We didn't want to stifle such a gift from God, **but** Mary had to learn to contain her music at times. We praised God for her abundant gifts, but brainstormed ways to find the external "off" switch while keeping Mary's internal music going. We had to practice.

One tool that helped was for Mary to listen to music through headphones while she studied, just as long as she didn't sing along in the classroom! That was a major compromise. Then we found that putting her verses and facts to music for her to use while she studied at home helped tremendously. (FYI: Most Bible verses can fit into one of the following tunes: "Joy to the World," "The Alphabet Song," "Jingle Bells," and "Holy, Holy, Holy." Try it. You'll be surprised at how easy it is!)

Use these strategies with music-smart kids.

✓ Let them use headphones and listen to music as they read and study.

✓ Allow them to sing their memory verses, rules, or facts they need to remember.

Interpersonal Intelligence: People Smart

These kids have great people-sense and discipline can best be accomplished through developing relationships with these children. They respond well to a "town hall"-type class meeting. These kids like to see the people part of discipline and readily respond accordingly.

Use these strategies with people-smart kids.

✓ Let them participate in peer-group counseling.

✓ Teach concepts of mutual respect.

✓ Allow time to be "social."

Intrapersonal Intelligence: Self Smart

These kids may be loners. You may have difficulty persuading them to participate in group activities. Yes, this child often responds to another drummer. Now to find that drummer…These children respond well if they feel you have respect for their individual styles. They enjoy talking with you one-on-one outside the classroom.

Use these strategies with self-smart kids.

✓ Give individual attention.

✓ Use behavior contracts.

✓ Allow time to work on high-interest projects.

In Conclusion...

Each of us is empowered when we feel "smart." Likewise, the energy drains from us when we feel "stupid." Affirming the "smartness" in each child will go far in preventing behavior problems. Teaching and disciplining to children's strengths helps them experience success, which is the greatest motivator of all.

4 Common-Sense Discipline Do's and Don'ts

Have your days on the earth been long enough that you remember the "Do Bees" and "Don't Bees" from *Romper Room,* a mid- to late-'50s children's TV show? Miss Somebody-or-other patiently taught that we "Do Bee kind," but that we "Don't Bee naughty;" that we "Do Bee polite," but that we "Don't Bee loud."

Well, we've put our heads together to give you a chapter of "Do Bees" and "Don't Bees" for children's workers in the church. These are discipline tips and tricks of the trade gleaned from our combined experience and study, deeply rooted in both the joys and the pitfalls of teaching God's children!

Portions of this chapter are photocopiable so that you may put these important basic principles of discipline into the hands of every children's worker in your church.

"Do Bee" Quick to Try These Desirable Discipline Devices!

As teachers, the way we approach our classrooms can make a world of difference in the amount and the kinds of discipline we need to apply. The wise teacher will implement as many preventive measures as possible as a way to stop discipline problems before they start. This is what we mean by training kids, discipling them, rather than simply handing out punishment when they don't act the way we think they should. Preventive discipline techniques provide a safe, comfortable, fair place for kids to learn about God. And these techniques also make your classroom a fun place to be.

🐝 **Do involve kids in making rules for your classroom.** On the first day of class, work with students to come up with three to five basic rules for the class. In one form or another, all the rules have to do with respecting God, the teacher, each other, and property. Involving students in this process makes them more aware of the rules, and because they've invested themselves in creating the rules, kids are much more likely to comply with them.

Do keep the rules simple and few. Classes can operate effectively with just these three simple rules.

1. If you want to talk, you may raise your hand and wait to be called on.

2. When someone else is talking, you may be quiet.

3. Keep your hands to yourself.

Do review the rules frequently. Every week start out by asking, "Now what are the rules for our classroom?" All the auditory students will blurt out: "I know! I know!" When that happens, say: "I want to hear you, but my ears only work when a hand is raised and I call on that person. I just have these silly ears. When a child talks out of turn, my ears don't work. Isn't that strange?"

For the visual students, you need to have the rules written and displayed on a wall. (See the photocopiable "Classroom Rules" poster on page 89.) Let tactual students and kinesthetic students make up actions or informal "sign language" to interpret the rules.

Do create a loving atmosphere where kids feel accepted "just the way they are." As adults, we'll do almost anything for someone who consistently shows us love and respect. The same holds true with children. The better the teacher-child relationship, the more likely it is that teachers will receive cooperation and respect when they direct children toward certain behaviors and tasks.

Do memorize the names of your students and use them frequently. We identify so completely with our names (or affectionate nicknames) that we feel a very warm, personal response when others call us by name or use our names in a positive way. Even though you may have children rotating in and out of your class, it's worth it to put in a little extra effort to learn each child's name.

If you're as forgetful as some of us are, you might want to have kids—or at least visitors—wear colorful name tags. Or let kids write their names in large letters on full sheets of paper. Take a photo of each child holding up his or her name. Create a class "lineup" on a bulletin board, or use the photos as flashcards. Keep a second set of prints in an envelope to share with substitute teachers and other class helpers.

Do remember that you're discipling children through discipline. That means that whatever we do as authorities in the child's life, we are serving as "dim copies" of Jesus himself. A good saying to remember is "God loves me just the way I am, and he loves me too much to let me stay that way." That's the same attitude children need to pick up from us—that we truly accept each child even as we challenge him or her to behave in a way that shows respect for God and for others.

⚜ Do be fair and consistent in dealing out consequences. There's no quicker way to start a confrontation than to give a child the feeling that you are being unfair. Children quickly lose heart if they feel that because the teacher doesn't like them, they are being treated differently than other kids. They also get confused when teachers say that the consequence for breaking a rule will be one thing but then assign a completely different consequence.

⚜ Do train children to be quiet when someone else has permission to speak. Talking out of turn may be the problem you'll deal with the most. While you can't make a child listen, you can make a child be quiet when someone else is talking.

For example, suppose you've called on Amy, and you are looking at her. Two girls on the other side of the room are thinking, "Teacher's looking over there; let's talk." Now you say, "Amy, just a minute," and you look at the other two. They may be so busy talking that they don't even realize you're looking at them.

So say: "We sure would like to hear what Amy has to say, but we can't because we have other people talking. I guess they've forgotten our rule that we're quiet when someone else is talking."

But the two chatterers are still going at it. You may have to walk all the way over to them. If you do that, try just to use your eyes and not repeat what you've already said. They'll get the message, one way or the other. If they aren't getting it, say: "We want to hear what Amy said. Amy raised her hand and I called on her. You may be quiet."

Then back away, but keep your eyes on the two talkers and move toward Amy. Maybe this seems like making a big deal out of a little issue, but if you let it go, the one conversation will become two, and two groups of kids talking will quickly become four. It's important to take care of the little things, because they can quickly escalate to big things.

⚜ Do "rove" the classroom. A teacher who walks around the classroom will encounter far fewer discipline problems than one who "stays put." If you're stationary, kinesthetic children will intentionally position themselves so that your view of them is obstructed. So will chatterers. Your proximity is important to keeping everyone involved with the lesson. And how much better to be close, to be giving eye contact and appropriate touch, than to be sitting at a desk barking orders!

⚜ Do confiscate little "treasures" that become a distraction. Use this little poem to teach kids what will happen if they bring "loot" to class to entertain themselves.

Bring your treasures to church;
That's fine.
But out of pocket or purse,
They're mine!

If you let children bring out their loot, they'll always be focused on the loot rather than the lesson. So if it comes out, it goes into a basket and kids can get it by coming back with Mom or Dad after church. Then you can explain the rule to Mom and Dad, which is good preventive discipline. If kids don't come back to reclaim their treasures, you can have a toy sale at the end of the year and give the money to the church.

Here's how to handle the confiscation of treasures with children of different temperaments. You're walking around and notice that Inspiring Ingrid has just taken out her lip gloss because she's tuned out the lesson and this little cosmetic gem seems a whole lot more interesting at the moment. She's an "I child," and you realize that she just "forgot" the rule. Remember, rule amnesia is prevalent among these children. The first time, you may give her the benefit of the doubt, but the second time the rule is broken, the lip gloss goes into the basket.

When you confiscate Dynamic Dan's Hot Wheels, you have to be a little stronger. Don't ever hurt a child, but use a firm touch and give him steady eye contact to remind him that you're still in charge. You may never retrieve anything from Steady Steve, because he only misbehaves behind your back. That's one reason to keep moving around the class—you don't want to have your back turned to Steady Steve for long periods of time!

❦ After a discipline scene, do reassure sensitive children that things are OK. Let's pretend we've just been through the confiscation of loot. Dynamic Dan is totally undaunted—it didn't phase him a bit. And Miss Inspiring Ingrid giggles and thinks this is fun. Steady Steve is grinning because, once again, he didn't get caught.

But Conscientious Connie over here is just not believing that this happened, and she's falling apart inwardly. Now she's not in trouble at all, but she's the one who's feeling the pain of all this. This is the child you need to reassure. Give her loving reminders that she's doing fine. Occasionally go over to this perfectionistic child and say: "Sweetheart, you're doing great. I'm so proud of you." You need to say that to this child because she simply won't know it if you don't say it.

You might be thinking, *of course she knows she's doing well—she didn't have anything confiscated. She never gets in trouble!* Remember, this child wants her world to be perfect, and it's not. So when you've disciplined someone else, remember to reassure Conscientious

Connie that things are OK. She's not the type of child who will walk up and give you a hug, but you need to make sure you hug her—she's the one who will remember it and cherish it more than any of the others.

⚙ Do use silent clues and signals to help active kids stay on task. Kinesthetic Ken has a lot of trouble containing himself in a chair. He's always on the verge of going into orbit with his hands and body. But you don't want to be calling his name all the time to tell him to settle down. You want the majority of your verbal messages to Ken to be positive, because being called on the carpet for his behavior is a way of life for this child.

Set up a system of clues and cues with Ken. Touch his hand or shoulder, pull on your earlobe, or even wink to let him know that it's time to haul back on the reins. If Ken is having a difficult day, pull him aside for a private conversation in the corner of the room. Better yet, if you have an assistant, take him for a little walk and talk. If you do go for a walk, stay in areas where you can be observed by others.

Tell Ken that you really think that God has made his body to enjoy moving. Has anybody ever said that to this child? No. They say, "What in the world is wrong with you?" Say to him: "When you need to move, I want you to know that I understand that. But when I'm teaching from God's Word, I need you to try as hard as you can to be really still. If I think you're forgetting, I may just stand by you and fold my hands. That's our special signal that I need you to fold your hands."

If he even gets the clue, that's progress. If he remembers to fold his hands, that's major progress. But keep giving him clues. If he keeps forgetting, go over and just touch his two hands together or hug him from behind and fold his hands. These gentle clues and reminders can go a long way toward helping this child—who's always in trouble—to stay out of trouble.

⚙ Do be a calming force in the classroom. When we move slowly, speak quietly but firmly, and move deliberately, our very presence calms overactive children. That's not to say that we always want our classrooms to be calm and sedate. Sometimes noise is good—the noise of learning, playing exciting games, and lively discussions. When we get loud, our kids will get loud—and if that's appropriate to the lesson, great! Then we need to let the kids know when it's time to be quiet again and enforce the quiet by our calm demeanor. Think of yourself as a peace that permeates the room. You are the calm in the storm, the oasis of quiet.

⚙ Do use attention-getting signals. Here's a great slogan for teachers: Don't yell—use the bell! When you raise your voice, the children's volume will automatically go up. When you speak quietly, children automatically quiet down so they can hear you. Too many teachers operate on high decibels. They yell every direction, they yell the Bible story, they yell disciplinary instructions—just to be heard above the hubbub. Then when they need to get kids' attention in an emergency, they have nowhere to go.

Here's a better plan: Use an attention-getting signal that kids will enjoy, such as a quiet, soft-toned bell, a low train whistle, or a party noisemaker. If you have a light switch nearby, you may want to flash the lights as an inaudible signal—in cramped quarters, other teachers might appreciate that consideration.

Once you've given the signal, don't start talking until you have every child's full attention. The last couple of kids to stop talking will get plenty of positive peer pressure to zip it up more quickly the next time. Make your signals fun, and change them from time to time. You may want to let kids loan their favorite noisemakers for a month's use as the classroom signal. Save your voice for the choir or the soccer game!

88 Do give children ample warning when it's time to move on to the next activity. We practice this as a natural courtesy with other adults. Imagine the annoyance if one spouse said to the other, "Stop what you're doing right now and come to dinner." Out of courtesy, we adults let each other know that it's ten minutes until dinner or that it's five minutes until we're ready to go. We need to exercise the same courtesy with children.

Make it a practice to warn your students when there are five minutes until they need to clean up the craft area. This allows them to quickly finish their projects or find a good stopping place. During interactive discussion, give students a one-minute or thirty-second warning rather than just cutting them off in the middle of a sentence. This is really a matter of respect. It helps kids learn to respect a schedule, and it teaches them the most basic aspects of time management. Giving kids cues about time remaining for an activity greatly reduces their frustration level and therefore reduces discipline problems.

88 Do find something to praise in each child. One teacher said, "The only thing I could praise was that he didn't go home with me." That doesn't count! Kids who are constantly reprimanded (and some are!) feel beaten up. We don't ever want children to leave our churches feeling defeated. Make an effort to praise every child at some point during every class. Verbal praise, a gentle touch, or a knowing wink of the eye can all be affirming to a child. When we affirm and cherish our students, we are modeling for them the kind and loving behavior that we're trying to help them develop.

&& **Do try to "get inside the head" of a child who requires constant discipline.** Carefully observe the child you are always having to discipline. It may be that this child doesn't get enough attention to satisfy his or her emotional needs. If you pay less attention when these children act out but lavish praise on their positive actions, the less desirable behavior may be extinguished as the child attempts to repeat the actions that garnered positive attention.

One year at camp, a girl attended who came from a strained family situation. Every time she went to a large-group activity, she'd trip or fall and be "injured" in some way. It got pretty annoying. The leaders thought she was "just being a baby." Finally it dawned on them that she was starving for attention and had learned to get "injured" in order to get an adult's sympathy. Once the leaders started downplaying our attention to the constant bumps and bruises and focusing lots of attention on everything else, the girl miraculously got less clumsy!

&& **Do mix children of various ages.** In the past few years, more and more schools around the country have experimented with multiage groups. This is really a return to the principles of the old-fashioned one-room schoolhouse. Mixing children of various ages allows kids to teach each other—a plus for both tutor and learner. The learner gets individual attention, and the tutor gets tons of interval reinforcement of the concepts he or she is passing along—it's the time-honored principle of the teacher being the one who learns the most.

Another positive aspect of the multiage class is that competition gives way to cooperation. That means that everyone operates at a more comfortable level and that kids are encouraging and helping each other instead of trying to "beat" each other. This cooperative spirit also greatly reduces discipline problems. Kids who are tutoring have no desire to cause discipline problems for themselves! Younger kids try to emulate the maturity of the older ones. Older kids do better when they realize that the little ones are looking up to them. The spirit of community that develops in the multiage classroom teaches kids to be caring and loving in their relationships.

&& **Do mix children of different genders.** Although this is a much-debated subject, boys and girls do better in mixed groups most of the time. On certain occasions and for certain topics, of course, it is wise to separate boys and girls and place them with adult leaders of the same gender. But in week after week of mixed classes, boys seem to have slightly better manners and self-control and girls tend to be a little sweeter and less chatty.

In fifth- and sixth-grade Sunday school, you can have the best of both worlds by having the large-group activities with all the boys and girls, small groups of mixed gender permanently assigned to one teacher for most small-group discussions, and various other groupings where boys and girls separate for a portion of the class. These changes keep children from being bored by the predictability of most classrooms. By eliminating boredom, we greatly reduce discipline problems.

❀ Do surprise kids with spontaneous celebrations for good behavior. Surprise your class after an exceptionally good day together. Keep a nonperishable treat stashed in your classroom and when that special day happens, break out the goodies. Be sure to be specific about all the good things the class did and said that day. This sort of surprise treat keeps kids from being good just for some sort of bribe. At the same time, it allows you to reinforce the positive behaviors that have happened in your classroom and lets your kids know that you're proud of them.

❀ Do offer kids choices, both in activities and in consequences. Kids appreciate having some sense of control, so the more opportunities you give them to make choices, the happier they will be. With happiness comes cooperation. Even if you don't have time to prepare two activities each week, you can ask the kids this week which of the activities they would like you to prepare for next week. This gets you started on lesson preparation right away, and it builds anticipation for the kids who have helped select their fun for next week!

When students misbehave, give them two choices: either behave appropriately or suffer the prescribed consequence. One common problem is when two friends want to sit together but they tend to chatter in private conversation rather than participating in class. Their desire to be together can work to your advantage. Tell them that it's a privilege, not a right, to sit with a friend. If they choose not to talk, they may stay together. If they choose to talk, they may sit apart. Either way, the choice is theirs. One pleasant byproduct of giving kids choices is that it takes the teacher out of the role of the "bad guy." Kids make choices, and kids are responsible for the outcome of their choices.

❀ Do work at finding special connections with challenging students. If you find yourself challenged by the same child repeatedly, you may need to talk to him or her outside of class. Once there was a two-year-old boy who apparently was rarely disciplined by his parents. He would constantly kick and hit other children and teachers. No matter what the teachers wanted him to do, he was determined to do something else. Finally, the teacher began greeting this child at the door and telling him how excited she was to see him, how much she loved him, and how she knew he was going to have a great day doing whatever the teacher wanted him to do and not kicking or hitting anyone. Surprise! His behavior began to improve!

Another tactic is to involve uncooperative older children in some aspect of teaching the class. Offer to let a child teach his or her favorite part of the lesson. It may seem risky, but the results can be very positive. Preparing part of the lesson gives a child ownership, and when kids have invested something in the lesson, they become supporters rather than detractors.

❀ Do be realistic in your expectations of your students. Review Chapter 2 from time to time to compare your class with the "norm." They're probably pretty typical. If you expect your students to be more mature than they are or to behave in ways that God has not wired them to behave, you and your students will be frustrated. Keep a prayer notebook with a page for each child. Write down positive steps you've seen each child make in your class as well as their specific needs. Take joy in every step a child makes toward God.

❀ Do be realistic in your expectations of yourself. In numerous surveys, both volunteer Sunday school teachers and full-time, paid preschool teachers were asked what topics they would like to see covered in teacher-training sessions. Guess what the number one topic is—discipline! No matter how much we learn and practice, we all need constant help in this area. Don't beat yourself up if your class isn't perfectly controlled every week. Take the good days when you get them. Remember, kids are works in progress. As a matter of fact, so are teachers. Be as patient with yourself as you are with your students. God isn't finished with any of us yet!

❀ Do rely on the power of prayer. If we hope to respond to our students in the spirit rather than in the flesh, we need to be before the Lord in prayer. There's just nothing like prayer! Write children's names on index cards and carry the cards with you to help you remember to pray for those children. All of us have children from time to time who are difficult for us to like; we love them in the Lord, but we'd just as soon not have them around. Pray for God to give you ways to bond with those children. When you pray for a child, so many times you'll find that God has done unusual and amazing things to draw you to that child—things that only God could orchestrate. God is faithful—pray and look for the answer.

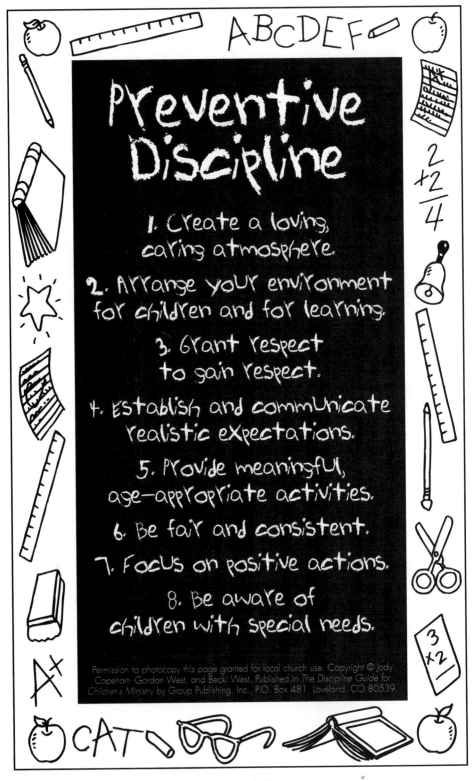

Preventive Discipline

1. Create a loving, caring atmosphere.

2. Arrange your environment for children and for learning.

3. Grant respect to gain respect.

4. Establish and communicate realistic expectations.

5. Provide meaningful, age-appropriate activities.

6. Be fair and consistent.

7. Focus on positive actions.

8. Be aware of children with special needs.

Classroom Rules

1. Use inside voices.

2. Raise your hand for permission to speak.

3. Be quiet when others are speaking.

4. Obey your teacher.

5. Visit the restroom before class begins.

6. Use good manners.

7. Keep your hands and feet to yourself.

"Don't Bee" Creating Discipline Problems for Yourself!

Why would I create problems for myself, you ask? Well you wouldn't—at least not on purpose. But occasionally we teachers unwittingly trip ourselves up. After all, teaching God's children is a complex business, and there is an enemy who would like to see us fail.

Check yourself against the "Don't Bees." If you don't see yourself on the list, congratulations! If you do, welcome to the human race. It never hurts to do a little self-evaluation. If nothing else, it can affirm all the things you're doing right!

🐝 **Don't use threats you can't or won't carry out!** Promising dire consequences that never materialize will only cause you to lose credibility with your students. An empty threat might be, "If you don't quiet down, we'll just sit here the rest of the morning." Resorting to threats lets kids know that they've pushed your buttons and that you're feeling powerless; otherwise, you wouldn't be making empty threats. Believe it or not, even preschoolers can figure this stuff out.

A teacher once told twenty two-year-old children, "If we can't be quiet for prayer, then no one will get a snack." Not only was this demand unrealistic (and unnecessary) for a classroom full of twos, but anyone watching knew immediately that, contrary to her threat, she was not going to punish the nineteen quiet children by taking away the snacks that were sitting right in front of them. If you start to make a threat like this, take a voluntary two-minute trip to the time-out chair to regroup. The kids will respect you for it!

When a teacher speaks in a threatening tone, kids will be quick to tune out the important things he or she has to say. You may want to run a "self-diagnostic" to find out how you sound to kids. A good way to do this is to tape-record a class. (Don't let all the little "hams" you're teaching discover that you're doing this!) Just set a little tape recorder in a corner of your classroom and let it run. As you play it back, listen to your tone as you're speaking to the kids. You may discover that you sound warm and pleasant, or you may find some areas to work on.

🐝 In the same vein, **don't yell at children, ever.** Yelling tells kids: she's outta control; he's lost it. Kids will quickly tune you out. On the practical level, there may someday be a serious situation in your classroom when you'll need to shout directions. Teachers who yell to be heard in every class don't have anywhere to go if the need arises. If you've been in the habit of shouting over kids' voices to be heard, first start using a signal such as a bell or a train whistle, and then consciously lower your voice. Kids will quickly learn that they need to be quiet in order to hear you.

🍀 Don't be late to class. There's an old adage about teaching: "Whoever gets to the classroom first is in charge for the whole morning." It's best that you, the teacher, are in charge of the classroom, so make it a point to get to the room first! Somehow children simply behave better when they are greeted by a calm, prepared teacher.

🍀 Don't come to class unprepared. How often have you tried to teach unprepared and found yourself nervous and tense throughout the class? Being prepared, preferably overprepared, gives you a confidence that your students will subconsciously pick up on. Good preparation also gives you the tools to flex with whatever the kids throw at you on any given day.

Lack of preparation creates small gaps in your lesson presentation as you search frantically through your notes for the next thing to do.

As part of your preparation, it's always wise to carry a few things with you into class—things that for some reason seem to disappear, such as tissues, glue sticks, and sharpened pencils. Otherwise, you may have to run and hunt up the necessary items. If you say, "I will be right back," the children do not look at each other and say: "Wow, the teacher is gone. Let us pause and reflect on how the Lord has worked in our lives this week." We know what we will return to! It takes only a few seconds for kids to find a new focus for the class— and it's not usually the focus you would choose!

🍀 Don't ever leave a class of preschoolers to go in search of supplies. It's amazing how quickly little ones can stage a coup, create a disaster, or otherwise bring the roof down around their ears. If you need someone to run an errand, call out to an older child or a helper from another class. Stay with those little guys—they need you every minute.

🍀 Don't give directions in the form of a question unless you are truly willing to let the children choose. When you ask the question "Would you like to sit down and listen to the Bible story now?" the child has every right to tell you: "No thanks, Teacher. I want to run around the room and scream." While no child would actually respond in those words (we hope), you can bet that one or two will demonstrate that answer in their behavior. If you want the children to sit down and listen, say, "It's time to sit down and listen."

This also applies for administering discipline. Don't ask the misbehaving child if she wants you to call her parents. Her answer, of course, will be negative. Instead, give her the choice of behaving or having you call her parents. When you give a child choices, make sure that you can live with the outcome. Keep the choices you offer within the realm of what's acceptable to you.

🎗 Don't interrupt activities for unrelated problems that can wait. For example, if the class is in the middle of a discussion and you stop them to ask if someone lost a coat, you will have created an unnecessary interruption. We adults don't like to be interrupted—kids don't either. When you shield your kids from interruptions, you're helping them focus on the lesson. Let little items of business wait until the end of class.

🎗 Don't handle severe problems alone. Having another adult with you will protect you from allegations of wrongdoing and will help you maintain your cool. For many years it was standard practice to take a child outside to deal with a discipline problem. In our lawsuit-prone society, that's no longer a good idea. You always need another adult as a support and a witness. In most classrooms, you can take a misbehaving child to one corner of the room, in full view of your other staff members, and talk privately without embarrassing the child or jeopardizing yourself.

If a child becomes very upset and a discipline situation escalates, get another adult involved immediately—preferably someone who's in charge. If the situation appears to be volatile, have the other adult take notes. This is the time to be "as smart as snakes and as innocent as doves" (Matthew 10:16). Be smart about protecting yourself and about preserving the child's dignity.

🎗 When children act out, don't ask "why" they did it. Most will have no clue as to how to answer the "why" question. It is a good idea, though, to ask the child what he or she did and what led up to his or her actions. These are questions that a child can answer; the questions will help you and the child reach an understanding about what needs to happen next in order for the child to get back on track.

🎗 Don't shame or blame a child. Shaming is easier to recognize than it is to define. Basically, any time a sense of scorn or scolding or a lack of forgiveness comes from an adult, a child feels devalued. What the adult needs to do is discuss the inappropriate behavior but make it clear that it's the behavior that's undesirable, not the child. After you've helped the child understand what was wrong with his or her behavior, it's important to give the child forgiveness and hope. Help the child understand and verbalize how to choose the right behavior next time, and express your confidence that he or she will do just that.

⽆ Don't label kids. At a recent teachers' meeting, one teacher brought up a family of brothers who have been a handful in their church's Sunday school classes over the years. This particular teacher was having problems with the middle child and wondered what to do. Another teacher quickly offered this advice: "You just need to sit on him, because all of those boys are 'that way.'" We need to guard ourselves against this kind of talk. It will set up negative expectations for every teacher down the line.

Each new class with a new teacher is an opportunity for a child to experience grace and to start fresh. We need to give kids chances to grow up. Some children do build reputations over the years, but who knows? The next teacher might be the very one who can help a child turn around. Instead of expecting the worst, let's stubbornly expect the best and realize that when we tap into the power of prayer, wonderful things can happen in a child's life.

Another pitfall to avoid is giving nonprofessional diagnoses of children's problems. Be wary of saying, "He's hyperactive" or "This child must have A.D.D." It is not up to the teacher to make these judgments or to ask a parent to put a child on medication. (If, however, a child has been diagnosed with a learning problem and takes prescription medication, it is fine to ask the parent if the child can be medicated on weekends.) Even if a child has been diagnosed with A.D.D., don't let that label be what you think of whenever he or she comes to mind. Kids with A.D.D. have their wonderful sides, too, as well as their good days.

Discipline Do's and Don'ts

Always...

- Reward attempts at positive behavior.

- Remain calm.

- Speak in a quiet, controlled voice.

- Deal with problem behavior one-on-one.

- Be flexible; go with the flow.

- Let child begin again with a clean slate.

No-No, Never-Never, Uh-Uh Uh!

- Shame and blame.

- "Blow your stack."

- Get involved in a shouting contest.

- "Chew out" a child in front of his or her peers.

- Create a confrontation or a standoff.

- Hold grudges.

Tips From the Trenches

Keeping a classroom under control can actually be fun—honest! Try these time-tested tips and techniques—they can do a lot of the work for you.

🎈 **The marble jar** provides a great incentive for good behavior. Many of your kids may already be familiar with it from their school classrooms. You'll need a large glass jar and a big bag of colorful marbles. Whenever you "catch" students staying on task, cooperating, being respectful, or demonstrating any other behavior you want to affirm, reach into the bag of marbles and put a handful of marbles into the jar. When the jar is full, congratulate the kids by letting them play a favorite game, giving them a special treat, throwing a party, or arranging a field trip. You may want to allow kids to vote on their choice of celebration options.

🎈 Use **paper chain-links** in a system similar to the marble jar above. When the class does well or a particular child does well with a new behavior, allow kids to add new links to a paper chain that's "growing" around the room. When the chain makes it all the way across a wall, surprise kids with a favorite game or activity. When it gets all the way around the room, throw a party!

🎈 Use these **rhymes and jingles** as attention grabbers and to help little ones through transitions.

- Form a pretty circle by the time I count to ten.
  (Children join in counting to ten.)

- Tiptoe, tiptoe oh-so-very slowly.
  Tiptoe, tiptoe oh-so-quietly.

- One, two, three, four,
  Watch us line up at the door!

- Wiggle your fingers,
  Point to the door.
  Stretch up high;
  Now sit on the floor.

- Put your hands together
  Just this way.
  Now we'll talk to God—
  Let's close our eyes and pray.

- How do we walk in the hall,
  In the hall, in the hall?
  We walk right up against the wall;
  We do it one and all!
  (to the tune of "The Mulberry Bush")

- Zip, zip, zip your lips
  In a great big smile.
  Now it's time to zip our lips
  And listen for a while.
  (to the tune of "Row, Row, Row Your Boat")

- Fold your hands, fold your hands;
  Do it now, you really can.
  We obey the teacher; yes, we do.
  You fold your hands, and
  I will too!
  (to the tune of "This Old Man")

The **time-out chair** is a useful technique in preschool, early-elementary, and middle-elementary classrooms. Use it when a child needs to be separated from the rest of the children to cool off, collect him or herself, and think about what it will take in order to rejoin the class successfully.

Place the time-out chair in a specific location, and let the kids know that this is the time-out chair and that it's only to be used for time-out. Help kids understand that the time-out chair isn't a punishment but a tool that helps them cool down, collect themselves, and refocus. For preschoolers, you might place a stuffed animal in the chair. For kids who can read, post a list of classroom rules (see the photocopiable "Classroom Rules" on p. 89) and the "Time-Out Checklist" from page 102 beside the chair.

Remember that children's attention spans are only one minute per year of age, so don't plan to leave them in the time-out chair for an eternity (which would be ten minutes or so for kids up through early elementary). For younger children, you may want to use an egg timer. When the sand runs out, they can rejoin the activity.

A better method, however, is to let kids decide for themselves when they're ready to rejoin the class. Explain that they'll know that it's time to come back when they've thought through their problem behavior and decided on a better way to behave. If it's obvious that they've returned to the action too quickly, gently say: "Anna, I wonder if you wouldn't benefit from a little more time in the time-out chair. Perhaps you didn't quite finish what you needed to do there."

If you send a child back to the time-out chair, plan to spend a few moments with the child. Point out the questions on the checklist poster, or guide a younger child through the process verbally.

When a child does rejoin the class successfully, be sure to acknowledge that success with a wink, a pat on the shoulder, or a whispered affirmation, such as, "Good job, Anna!"

The **colored-card system** is another great behavior modification technique. This works best in a classroom where the same children attend regularly. Each child has an envelope with his or her name written on it. It's best to place the envelopes in a private place, such as in a workbook, a cubby, a desk, or at the student's work area. (Some teachers place the cards on a wall, but we feel that this is too punitive for some children.) Each envelope contains a green card, a yellow card, and a red card. When class begins, the green cards are on top, signifying that everything is "go!"

When Jason misbehaves, the teacher asks him to go to his envelope and place the green card in the back of the envelope, exposing the yellow "caution" card. If Jason acts out again, the teacher asks him to place the yellow card in the back and expose the red card. The red card may indicate loss of a privilege or a logical consequence of the offending behavior.

The **balloon-pop system** is great fun and avoids singling out individual children. Blow up several balloons, attach strings to them, and hang them from the ceiling in a colorful "balloon bouquet." Whenever a child misbehaves, the teacher pops a balloon. The loud pop reminds everyone to stay on task and the child who was "caught" scurries back to the job at hand, thankful that he or she wasn't pointed out to the rest of the class!

The **bell signal** "rings in" order in just a few amazing moments. Ring a bell gently just once. Train children to listen and respond quickly. By the time the vibrations of the bell fade to silence, the children have to close their mouths, put their hands behind their backs, put their feet on the floor, turn their eyes to you, and freeze. They remain frozen until you quietly say, "Defrost." Defrost means that they can get into relaxed positions, but there's still no talking until you call on someone. To make it playful, defrost kids one by one by tapping them on their heads or shoulders.

A little **role reversal** can do wonders. Let volunteers prepare and teach part of a lesson. Once kids have experienced how challenging it is to be the teacher, chances are that they'll be ready to give the real teacher a break! This works well only if the participants really want to give it a try.

● The **Wheel of Scripture game** is a terrific motivational tool to keep kids in grades three through six on their best behavior. Say, "If we can get through our lesson and clean up our room with everyone participating and cooperating, we'll have time at the end to play Wheel of Scripture." Make a wheel and a spinner from poster board, or use a die or a spinner from another game.

Write out a Bible verse with each letter on a separate self-stick note. Arrange the letters on a wall or board with the blank sides of the notes toward the kids.

Form two teams, and have them take turns spinning the spinner. When the spinner lands on a number, the team guesses that many consonants or vowels. If those letters are in the verse, turn the papers with those letters over and give that team another turn. If the letters they call out aren't in the verse, the other team gets a turn. The object of the game is to be the first team to guess the entire verse.

● Kids love to receive surprise **showers of blessings** as positive reinforcement for a great day or for putting forth good effort on a difficult project. Keep a little stash of tiny treats. When you want to say "Good job, kids," simply call out "Heads up!" and then toss handfuls of treats into the air. Encourage children to share as they gather their goodies so everyone gets an approximately equal amount.

● **Flashing the lights off and on** is a silent but very effective way of grabbing kids' attention and letting them know that the decibel level is getting to be painful.

● **Dim the lights** on a day when children are bouncing off the walls. Instead of using bright overhead lights, use natural light from a window or a lamp with a soft glow. Because light is a stimulus, lack of light helps create a calmer atmosphere.

● Thirty seconds of **silly exercise** is a great way to help kids get the wiggles out. Call out orders similar to these:
● Stretch your arms overhead and try to tickle the stars.
● Lean over from the waist and wave through your legs at someone behind you. (Skip this one if girls are in dresses.)
● Shake your head back and forth and try to make your cheeks wiggle.

- Shake out your arms.
- Shake out your middle.
- Shake out your right leg.
- Shake out your left leg.
- Shake out both legs (which they can't do because they're standing up—but it gets a good giggle).
- Drop to the floor and sit up tall.
- Deep breath in…blow it out. (Repeat this three or four times, but "forget" to tell them to blow it out the last time—just for a couple of extra seconds.)

Kids love this routine no matter how many times you do it. Vary it a bit each time. After their deep breaths, they'll be ready to focus again on the lesson.

🎈 Here's a great **wiggle-eraser** for little ones. Sing it to the tune of "Ten Little Indians." Have kids wiggle the appropriate number of fingers as they sing and then hide their fingers behind their backs.
One little, two little, three little wiggles;
Four little, five little, six little wiggles;
Seven little, eight little, nine little wiggles;
Ten little wiggles are gone.

🎈 When kids are sluggish or tired, use the beloved old **beanbag** to keep them on their toes. When you're going over a memory verse, calling out quick-response questions, or reviewing lesson material, have children raise their hands if they know the answer or the next word. Toss the beanbag to a child with his or her hand up; he or she tosses it to another child for the next word or answer, and so on. Have kids who've already answered keep their hands down until everyone has had a turn. Kids will focus and participate because they each want to have a turn.

🎈 Use the **say, sign, and sing** method to put classroom rules or procedures in a fun, easy-to-remember format. Use familiar tunes such as "The Alphabet Song," "Twinkle, Twinkle, Little Star," "Jingle Bells," or "Yankee Doodle." You can make up your own informal hand-motions or refer to a sign language book that will help you with simple signs. This works for all learners because they **see** it, **do** it, and **hear** it simultaneously. Mega input!

🎈 Children love the **"Tremendous Tree."** Have kids help you make a tree trunk and branches by twisting brown-paper grocery bags and taping them to a wall. As a time stuffer, let kids tear leaf shapes from different shades of green construction paper and tape the leaves to the tree. Cut large red apples from construction paper. Write each child's name on an apple, and let children attach their apples to the tree. When a child cooperates, obeys, or tries, put a smiling worm on his or her apple. Look for something positive to praise in each child each week.

● Here's another **wiggle-taming song.** Sing it to the tune of "If You're Happy and You Know It."

If you really love Jesus, take a stand.
If you really love Jesus, spin around.
If you really love Jesus, jump up and down.
If you really love Jesus, sit down!
(whisper) Don't make a sound!

Say: "What good listeners you are—I'm so proud of you! I guess I'll have to think of a harder song for next week."

(Warning: Use this song only with children age seven or younger—with older kids it will get you tarred and feathered!)

● With some children, **simple contracts** with incentives for good behavior may work wonders. You may photocopy the contracts on page 103 for use with your children. On the first contract, write in one or two desired behaviors, such as:
- keeping my hands to myself,
- listening when others are speaking,
- raising my hand before I speak, and
- being kind to others.

● **Puppets** love to lend a hand with discipline. They can whisper in a child's ear, "When you talk loudly, it scares me and I want to run away," "I've seen how nicely you've been sharing the crayons today," or "I think that new little girl looks lonely. Would you come visit her with me?" Children will often receive a message from a puppet when they might brush off the same message from an adult.

● **People placement** can be a key factor in bringing out the best in a group of kids. Place children according to their needs.

- Keep active children near you. You can refocus them by gently squeezing their hands. When they're near you so that you can do this easily, they will get the physical reminder and the pleasant reinforcement of your gentle touch without being embarrassed by constant verbal reprimands.

● Put quiet kids across the circle from you where you'll have direct eye contact. Whoever sits across from the leader of the group naturally gets more eye contact and, therefore, more nonverbal permission to talk. This is encouraging to the nontalker and may be just what the child needs to get involved in the discussion.

● Place talkative children out to the side, at the three o'clock and nine o'clock positions in a circle. Kids who may dominate conversations or seek too much of your attention will not receive as much eye contact in these positions, and, therefore, will receive fewer nonverbal cues that it's OK to speak.

● Explain to "chatty" friends that sitting together is a privilege. Make it clear that one reminder to stop talking will mean that they'll need to sit apart.

● Use **tick-tack-toe** with middle- to upper-elementary kids when you're working on a specific behavior such as raising hands or cleaning up quickly. Prepare a tick-tack-toe grid on poster board or on a large piece of flannel. Cut out X's and O's of the same material. Any time you want to reinforce positive behavior, say, "We're on for tick-tack-toe." Organize teams. When you catch a child following a rule without being told, that person's team can add an X or an O to the board. This creates a fun atmosphere of positive peer pressure as the kids begin to monitor each other.

Time-Out Checklist

This is a place for you to rest and
get ready to rejoin the class.

1. Take several deep breaths
to help you relax.

2. How are you feeling right now?

3. Why are you feeling that way?

4. What choice did you make that
brought you to the time-out chair?

5. What would have been a better choice?

6. What choices do you need to make
in order to rejoin the class successfully?

7. When you feel calm and ready to
follow our rules, you may rejoin the class.

_____
(child's name)

Date_____

I will do better at

_____

_____

_____.

Signed _____
(teacher)

_____
(child)

_____
(parent)

_____
(child's name)

Every time I get ____ stars on my card, I will earn

_____.

Signed _____
(teacher)

Date _____

Remedial Discipline

No matter how well-prepared you are, no matter how faithfully you love and pray for your kids, no matter how thoroughly you understand the philosophy of discipline and discipling, there will be trying moments in your classroom. So expect them—don't wail, rent your garments, or gnash your teeth. Kids will be kids and teachers are just human. So when a child goes ballistic, a seemingly innocent game backfires, or the wheels fall off, here's what to do.

● **Respond—don't react.** When we *react,* we are in the flesh. What we want to do is *respond* in the power of the Holy Spirit. Move slowly toward the child and pray as you go. This is the Christian version of counting to ten!

● **Be empathetic.** Approach the unruly child with the attitude that you'd like to know what is going on in his or her mind so you can help. Say, "It seems like you're having a rough time today—can I help?" This is a polite way of telling the child that you expect better behavior than that which you just witnessed.

You might say: "Maybe you'd feel better if you sat out for a while. You can rejoin us when you're ready." This isn't a blaming statement, but it points out the problem. It gives a child permission to sit out and return in his or her own time. This respectful direction helps most kids take responsibility for their actions.

● **Don't take it personally.** An episode of acting out may be the result of what happened in a child's life an hour or a day before you came into contact with him or her. Lots of us are quick to blame ourselves. Don't. Consider the metaphor of the windshield and the bug. (Not quite as lovely as the lilies of the field, is it?) The windshield may take a hit, but only because it was there. It didn't provoke the bug, nor was the bug aiming for it. Sometimes teachers take hits just because they're there. Don't worry about the provocation. Realize that your role is to help the child put his or her world back together.

● **Defuse the situation before it becomes a confrontation.** A confrontation is *always* a lose-lose situation. No one likes to be backed into a corner. The goal of discipline is not to control but to be skilled guides and facilitators who help children learn to know, love, and follow Jesus.

Two new girls came to an outreach event for fifth- and sixth-graders. They were antagonistic and disrespectful. As the other students listened to instructions, these two kept giggling and talking. The situation became tense. Finally, the leader confronted them in front of the group and asked them to step to the back of the room to talk with another staff member. A better plan of action would have been to talk to the girls personally in a low voice, giving them a choice rather than an ultimatum. As it was, the leader lost some of his credibility with the whole group and the two girls remained belligerent.

● **Treat the misbehaving child with respect.** Boy, is it tempting to "let 'er rip!" Don't do it. Your job is to build up the child. By remaining polite, you don't allow the child to pull you into the "bad guy" role.

Pull the child aside and deal with him or her individually rather than in front of the class. By doing this, you take the child out of the "limelight." Some kids simply won't bother to act out if there's no audience!

One substitute teacher found this principle to be true. He discovered that children would gladly ham it up when confronted in class, because they figured they could push his buttons and that the whole class would back them up. He found that a polite, one-on-one conversation with the student took away the desired audience. By treating the child with respect, a teacher helps the child calm down. That makes it easier for the child to move from belligerence to cooperation.

● **Make sure that the child understands why his or her behavior was unacceptable.** It's important for the child to be able to verbalize what it was that he or she did wrong and to understand why that behavior is not allowed in your classroom. Not long ago, a teacher disciplined a child in children's church for throwing something. When the teacher asked the child if he knew what he had done, the child said, "No, but the guy sitting next to me threw something" (and the child was right). Even though the teacher was embarrassed, he was grateful that he'd given the child a chance to set him straight.

Kids need to understand what it is that they're being disciplined for. Vague discipline creates confusion, frustration, and probably more open rebellion in the future.

One of the writers of this book—who shall remain anonymous—experienced this confusion firsthand. I was stopped by a traffic policeman. I pulled over obediently, but I had no idea what could have caused that officer to turn on his lights. As I fished for my license, title, and proof of insurance, I wracked my brain but failed to come up with anything. The officer found my paperwork to be in order and then asked, "Do you know why I pulled you over?" "No!" I replied. He explained that he'd pulled several people over just to explain that one side of the intersection has a turn lane while the other does not. "Lots of people have nearly turned into oncoming traffic and that nearly happened to you. I'm not going to ticket you today," he said. "I just want you to be safe in the future."

Isn't that exactly what we want for our kids? When the teacher bears down with that "Now you're in trouble" look, the targeted child may be just as confused as I was. So first, we need to get the facts—it could be that what we thought we saw wasn't what actually happened at all. In those situations we need to follow the example of the kindly patrolman and show mercy.

● **Make sure the child understands the consequences of his or her behavior.** When you were growing up, did you ever have a teacher or parent say, "I haven't decided what to do with you yet"? The dreaded delayed sentence. Kids don't perform well while sitting under a thundercloud. Justice needs to be swift and fair. Whether it's revocation of a privilege, a few minutes in the time-out chair, an apology to be given, or a visit to the church office, just do it! (You don't even need that little Swoosh on your shoes.) Some of us are experts at giving the silent treatment. Uh-uh, nope, no way, not in God's church. Levy the consequences and then forgive and bring out that clean slate.

● **Immediately redirect the child to a new activity.** The natural consequence of not using scissors correctly is to lose the privilege of using the scissors for the remainder of the day. That doesn't mean that the child needs to be excluded from enjoying the rest of the class. Give the child the option of going to one of two other learning centers. Get him or her back on a positive track and reinvolved in the lesson.

● **If the situation is a serious one, bring closure and new direction by creating a behavior contract.** No one child can be allowed to spoil a class for the rest of the children or the teacher. If a child continues to act out, consider meeting with the parents and the child and working together to create a behavior contract that all parties will sign. (See the sample contracts on page 103.) Carefully think through what behaviors the child needs to change. Include positive incentives in the contract. Make sure the child gets a copy of the contract. Set up a date to review the contract together. Once you've taken this step, reassure the child of your confidence that he or she can turn things around.

● **Cover the situation with prayer.** This is obviously the most important discipline tool of all, but it's easily overlooked. The kids in our classes are God's kids. We are the tools, but the work is God's.

When we pray, we open ourselves to change. Two teachers experienced this with two girls in their church. The girls were consistently misbehaving. They became a real bother for the adult workers, who started to develop an attitude about these two children. They finally realized they needed to pray for the girls. It was only then that the teachers were convicted to learn more about these girls. They discovered that the girls' home situation was difficult. Shortly after the teachers had begun to pray, the girls' mother was late picking them up after an all-nighter. While waiting for the mom to arrive, the teachers realized that the girls' time at church was the only positive time in their lives. Now there's a purpose to the time spent with these two girls, and the teachers' patience with them seems to be growing.

● **Keep your perspective.** Today's class was a bummer? Next week will be better. You are part of the pattern of love that God is weaving into the lives of the children you teach. The pattern may seem ragged at times, but we are all "works in progress." Remember, kids will be kids, and most kids will eventually attempt to push you to your limit. As you enforce rules lovingly and fairly, you teach children that they're secure. Kids in your care don't need to worry about the universe because a caring adult has this corner of it under control. When kids know they're safe in your love, you've done your job.

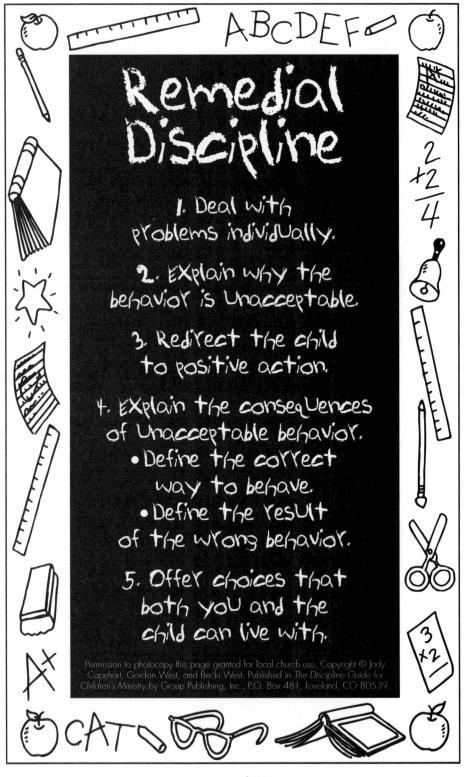

Remedial Discipline

1. Deal with problems individually.

2. Explain why the behavior is unacceptable.

3. Redirect the child to positive action.

4. Explain the consequences of unacceptable behavior.
   - Define the correct way to behave.
   - Define the result of the wrong behavior.

5. Offer choices that both you and the child can live with.

5 The Extra Challenge—
Kids With A.D.D.

Attention Deficit Disorder continues to be a subject that is widely misunderstood. We went from a lack of knowledge about A.D.D. to an abundance of knowledge, and we're now at the point where everyone is tired of hearing about it! A.D.D. does exist, but not in the epidemic proportions that we've seen being diagnosed in the last few years. Where does the truth lie?

The Whats and Whys of A.D.D.

Let's begin with the basics. A.D.D. is a neurological disorder that is usually transmitted genetically. Please note that A.D.D. is the generally used name that includes both A.D.D. (without the hyperactivity factor) and A.D.H.D. (with hyperactivity). It is characterized by distractibility, impulsiveness, and restlessness. These symptoms are present from childhood with a much greater intensity than in the average person, to the point that they may interfere with day-to-day functioning. A more descriptive name for Attention Deficit Disorder might be **attention inconsistency,** because even children with A.D.D. can learn to focus when they're motivated, confident, and involved in an active-learning environment that addresses their need to move and touch.

What exactly is the neurological problem that causes this disorder? Let's take a clinical look and then translate that into a word picture. One of the functions of the human brain—particularly the two cerebral hemispheres—is to coordinate, moderate, direct, and integrate all of the input to and output from the brain. Included in these functions is the process of mediating attention span, imposing control, and managing all of the sensory stimuli that bombard the brain. The brain carries out this process through an elaborate system of communication between the brain cells that is facilitated by chemicals called **neurotransmitters.**

These neurotransmitters enable the brain cells to communicate with each other in order to coordinate and organize functions and behavior. Empirically, we know that children with attention deficit disorders have some sort of dysfunction with this neurotransmitter system, probably a slight deficit in production of neurotransmitters. When the level of the neurotransmitters is lowered, the brain has difficulty carrying out its functions of maintaining attention span, screening out sensory distractions, and organizing impulse control. It's easy to see how that dysfunction leads to the behaviors we commonly see in kids with A.D.D.

> Every teacher and parent who works with a child with A.D.D. needs to bear this in mind: A.D.D. is not primarily an emotional problem but rather a neurological problem with a biological basis and behavioral manifestation.

Using a visual metaphor, we can think of the brain in terms of a huge dot-to-dot picture. The dots represent neurotransmitters. Picture a baby who is learning to walk. The child falls and gets up, falls and gets up countless times. But the child is determined! Each repetition of falling and getting up "connects the dots." If babies gave up each time the dots failed to connect, they would never learn to walk. It is a building process—one that feeds on success. We need to help children with attention deficits connect the dots more readily by coaching their efforts in incremental steps, by mentoring them through the discipline process, and by applauding appropriate behavior. Praise, repetition, and success help to connect the dots.

What Are Little Boys Made Of?

A.D.D. with hyperactivity appears to be more frequent than A.D.D. without hyperactivity. There are eight to ten boys for every girl with the disorder. The reason for this sex discrepancy has to do with fetal brain development. Because of the natural changes that occur in the male fetal brain, it seems to be more vulnerable to the neurological differences that lead to A.D.D.

What is the general nature of boys? They are more physical—their play is often rougher and rowdier than that of girls. They tend to communicate in sounds rather than words when they play. Even without A.D.D., boys appear to have more of the characteristics of A.D.D. simply because of their biological makeup. When we teach these young-men-in-the-making to appropriately harness their energy, they will be great workers for God's kingdom!

Let's look at how our culture contributes to the problem. Years ago, when boys ran three miles to school, ran three miles home, and then did chores, this energy was seen as an asset. Contrast that with a typical day in our modern culture. Children get driven to school, picked up from child-care, taken to competitive sports practices or games, and then driven home where they'll probably sit for hours doing homework or watching TV. There is little natural outlet for all of their energy, so the energy overflow spills out into the classroom where it's interpreted as a discipline problem.

The Diagnosis of the Decade

One main concern is that the majority of children who are diagnosed with A.D.D. today do **not** have A.D.D. So many children are diagnosed with A.D.D., but the accurate percentage should be around three percent of all children; out of that percentage, about eighty to ninety percent are boys. What's happening? Why the increase in the diagnosis of A.D.D.?

> I believe that A.D.D. has become the "Diagnosis of the Decade." Children are like sponges—they absorb the world around them. And like mirrors, they reflect it back. The message that children are reflecting back to us today is that the world has gone crazy.

The pace of life is too hectic, there are no boundaries for quiet times, and the family does not have enough time to simply be home and quietly absorb the beauty of God's world around them. We have stores open twenty-four hours a day and noise from phones, faxes, cellular phones, TV, and boomboxes coming at us constantly. This phenomenon in our culture results in children who bounce off the walls— and who are misdiagnosed with A.D.D. Until we s-l-o-w d-o-w-n as a culture in general and as a family in particular, the false symptoms of A.D.D. will continue to appear.

It Doesn't "A.D.D." Up!

Much of the misdiagnosis of A.D.D. can be attributed to the misunderstanding of learning differences or personality traits. Chapter 3 dealt with those differences. When you look at the symptoms of A.D.D., it's easy to understand how many personality and perceptual characteristics may be mistaken as A.D.D.

For example, when we look at personality types, we see that the D (dominant, dynamic) child—our Dynamic Dan from Chapter 3— needs to control everyone and every situation around him. Dan may appear to have A.D.D., but what we're really seeing is a dominating temperament.

The I (influencing, inspiring) child—Inspiring Ingrid—loves everyone and may be very talkative. This eager-to-talk nature may be misinterpreted as A.D.D.

Let's consider perceptual strengths or modalities—the way children take in information. The auditory child may talk a lot, interrupt, and ask a zillion questions in order to complete the learning loop in his or her mind. These are all characteristics of A.D.D. as well and may be a source of misdiagnosis. The tactual child needs to touch and manipulate in order to learn; the kinesthetic child needs to move a lot—both of these modalities can be readily misunderstood as A.D.D.

As I have trained teachers around the country, I have been increasingly alarmed at the number of children who are on medication for what may appear to be A.D.D. One blue-ribbon, award-winning school district had thirty-two percent of their kindergarten children on medication! This hurts my heart, because in kindergarten, it is developmentally *normal* to move! To me, medicating these children is a crime against childhood.

Characteristics of A.D.D.

Until very recently, there has been no objective diagnosis for A.D.D. There has been a list of characteristics. Children who demonstrate several of these characteristics are diagnosed with A.D.D., thus making the greater part of the diagnosis subjective. The list of characteristics is given below. As you read through them, don't be surprised if you find yourself on the list. Wow! Does that mean you have A.D.D.? No, it means you are a human being; in the flesh we all have many of these qualities. It's just human nature! If a child has A.D.D., he or she will demonstrate seven to fourteen of these characteristics on a day in, day out basis.

● The child may or may not be hyperactive. A.D.D. often stands for A.D.H.D. as well.

● A.D.D. is a neurological dysfunction. The brain is not sending messages back and forth in a normal way from one area of the brain to another. One area that doesn't receive the right message is the area of the brain that controls behavior—so we see inappropriate behavior. The medication, in this case, becomes the chemical that helps the neurotransmitters syntax properly, thus facilitating better communication within the brain.

● The child may have a short attention span.

● The child is easily distracted, but so are a lot of children who are bored.

● They are usually impulsive. When you ask them why they did something, their answer is always "I don't know," and they really don't know!

● Thus, their behavior is often very inappropriate.

● They are inconsistent. One day they can do it and the next day they can't. One day they know it and the next day they don't. This is frustrating for the adult as well as for the child.

● They have difficulty building cumulative memory. Most of us over forty have had the experience of walking into a room to get something, forgetting why we are there and walking out, only to remember again; going back in and forgetting again…it's so frustrating! We feel really stupid! This is what it *feels* like to have A.D.D. **Information moves in and out, seemingly out of the child's control.** It is *not* a factor of intelligence—many kids with A.D.D. have very high IQs. It's simply a problem of building cumulative memory.

● They have difficulty in schoolwork which is left-brain (it puts small parts together into the whole), since most children with A.D.D. function **best** from the right sides of their brains. They **can** operate from both sides, but the right side is where they're most comfortable when processing new information.

● They can do only one task at a time. When we say, "Put away your Bible and come to the worship center," they often get off task. Why? They need to be given one instruction at a time, or they'll go into overload.

"The Lord caused me to lie down in green pastures once, and I got in big trouble for getting grass stains on my good clothes."

• They can be argumentative and angry, usually because this is how they perceive others to be. They miss the normal behavioral clues that warn most kids that the adult is getting upset with them. As a result, they're always experiencing the anger of others.

• They have dramatic mood swings.

• They're often disorganized.

• They have a low stress tolerance. They don't see how the things they do all day such as fidget, chatter, and make noises are annoying to others. But when a normal behavior (such as a sneeze) comes from another child, they become very upset. It's one of the ironies of A.D.D. Kids with this disorder distract others, but they cannot take any distraction from others.

• They blurt out their thoughts without permission, talk excessively, and interrupt on a regular basis. Yet so do auditory children in many cases.

• They often lose things, but so does the I child.

• They have trouble in social situations because they miss the normal social cues.

• They want instant gratification, which is why computer games are so appealing to them (and also "A.D.D.ictive," I might "A.D.D.").

• They often shift from one unfinished activity to another.

> "A.D.D. kids are normal kids who do
> normal things more intensely"
> (Dr. Paul Warren).

In terms of education, children with A.D.D. typically have trouble with the mechanics of reading, comprehension, spelling, punctuation, and the basic mechanics of language, because these are left-brain strengths and these children are often stronger in right-brain activities.

When we use the phonics approach to teach reading, we go from parts of a word to the whole word. For a child with A.D.D. who is often more right-brain, going from parts to a whole does not build the cumulative memory necessary in order for him or her to remember the parts and deduct the whole. Thus, it may be better for this child to see the **whole word** first—or the whole of anything first. (Don't worry! We are not advocating whole language, only using the whole word.)

To put it simply, many kids can look at the parts of something and put it together in their minds. That's sequential thinking. Sequential thinkers follow the step-by-step drawings to put a complicated toy together. Most kids with A.D.D., on the other hand, need to see the whole of something before they can understand the parts. They tend to be global thinkers. They'll study and puzzle over the picture of the completed toy until the light bulb goes on. Then they'll put it together, sometimes more efficiently than the kids who are working step-by-step!

When a child with A.D.D. sits puzzling over a sequential task, struggling with how to begin, it's easy for a teacher to misunderstand the fact that the child is "stuck" and interpret his or her behavior as stubbornness or defiance. Put yourself in the shoes of "A.D.D. Adam." When all the children around him are working away, he's sitting there in frustration (and sometimes despair!), realizing that this is yet another task that won't be done on time, knowing that the teacher sees him as a problem and that he's about to be in trouble again. More A's for the kids all around him, more D's and F's for him. More admonitions to try harder. Multiply that scenario by the five to ten (or more!) times that it might happen during a school day and then multiply that by the number of school days in a year.

These children are precious in God's sight! They desperately need our unconditional love, understanding, encouragement, and approval. If one child with A.D.D. can create so much frustration around himself or herself, imagine the frustration level inside the child.

What Kids With A.D.D. Need From Us

The best way to deal with children with A.D.D. is to **direct** and **redirect** them. Because of their distractibility and impulsiveness, they easily get off task. A gentle, loving reminder is what these children need to get back on track. And no, you don't need to give a lecture. Sometimes you don't even need to speak—a touch on the shoulder or hand may be enough.

One challenge that faces Christian education workers is dealing with children with A.D.D. who are on medication during the week and then off the medication on the weekends. There has been concern that medicating these children all week long isn't good for them, but the latest research is stating that children *can* stay on most medications during the weekend. This will certainly make a difference in your Sunday school class *if* the child does need medication. You may want to check with the parents.

Most children with A.D.D. need structure, and the weekend is when structure is least likely to occur. On weekends children may visit the noncustodial parent. They may have sleepovers where they do anything but sleep. They may have sporting events all Saturday. In addition, children often eat lots of junk food on Saturdays. On Sundays, we see the result.

What is the solution? **Structure, consistency,** and **patience.** Sunday morning may be the only time a child feels welcomed, loved, and appreciated. What a great foretaste of knowing the Savior and of heaven! As Sunday school teachers, we need to get above the hurried hassle of our responsibilities and realize that we have the God-given opportunity to impact lives for eternity! What a privilege it is to bring these children to Jesus.

ABCs of Action!

Let's look at some methods and mind-sets that help a child with A.D.D. function better in the classroom as well as at home. These methods would apply to any other child as well, but they are especially helpful for the child with A.D.D.

A: Assist in short-term goals. Define easy-to-reach goals so these kids can begin to experience success. Don't try the delayed gratification technique of "You did so well today. I know you can do it! If you do as well for the next three Sundays, I'll have a special surprise for you." Guess what? You just set the child up for failure. Take a good day when you get it. It is a gift. Celebrate it!

B: Believe in them. This will do more than anything to help children with A.D.D. They tend to be relational, and they're often lonely. When you focus on building a positive relationship, many discipline issues can be resolved through the vehicle of the relationship.

C: Cues and clues. When you meet with children with A.D.D. in private (which they love!), suggest a secret system of **cues and clues** that you can use to get them back on the appropriate track without embarrassing them. For example: If you see A.D.D. Adam going into orbit, pull on your ear. He may miss that subtle clue. Level two may be that you go stand by him. Don't glare down at him, just gently make your presence known. The third may be a bearhug from the back that allows you to gently fold his hands together. The point is that if he understands that you want to help him, he will begin to trust your signals. You are simply making him aware of his behavior and helping him learn to harness all the energy that's pouring through his body.

D: Discipline. Discipline these children by **directing** and **redirecting** them back to the appropriate tasks and behaviors.

E: Empower them through the environment. Children with A.D.D. are very sensitive to the environment. They get overstimulated by too many things going on around them. Seat them where there is a minimum of distractions. Realize that they need active learning but that, at a certain point, it may overstimulate them. Help them find things to work on alone to keep them from being overly stimulated by the other children. Remember that they work best with soft light and on the floor. Taking them away from being directly under a fluorescent light will help a great deal.

F: Frequent breaks. Give kids with A.D.D. frequent breaks. They simply can't sit still and listen for long periods of time. (Most children can't, but children with A.D.D. find it especially difficult.) When there is an extended listening time, encourage them by saying: "I'm so proud of how you are trying to stay still. In five minutes we're going to move around. Please hang in there with me for just five more minutes." This encourages children with A.D.D. because they fear having to sit still for extended periods of time.

G: Give clear instructions, and give only one instruction at a time. Children with A.D.D. rarely fail to follow instructions out of willful disobedience but rather because they are in overload.

H: Hands-On. Kids with A.D.D. calm down with hands-on activities. Even at break time, set out manipulatives they can touch and enjoy.

I: Instruct children in self-monitoring. Children with A.D.D. are often completely unaware of the impact they have on others. In private, gently suggest that when they make tapping sounds on the table (or sound effects, or burping—the list goes on and on), it may be annoying to others. Brainstorm more appropriate uses of their hands and mouths to help them begin to do self-talk to manage their behavior. By the way, they can't hear these words from you unless they truly believe you love them and respect who they are as individuals. Like all children, they have selective hearing.

J: Jokes and humor. Children with A.D.D. usually have good senses of humor. They just don't want to be the brunt of jokes and humor any more than the rest of us do. But you can use humor to help them get past an uncomfortable time. For example, I have asked a child on a particularly "kinesthetic" day, "By any chance, did you eat wiggle worms for breakfast today?" They get the message without you having to give a lecture about wiggling.

K: Kindness. Be kind to children with A.D.D. They often feel that nobody wants them around (and yes, it is often true). Because they miss the normal behavioral clues, they don't know why people aren't kind to them. They soak up kindness the way a person soaks up water on a hot day.

L: Love. Love them, love them, and love them again. If you can't find the love in your heart, pray for God to give it to you.

There was a child I was honestly having trouble loving. I guess you could say I "loved him in the Lord," but I was weary of him in the flesh! We'll call him Fred. I had really been praying about this, which, of course, is the answer to all of our problems! We just tend to forget about the Lord's help and try to solve our problems on our own.

One thing to note about children with A.D.D. is that they are rarely late, they never get sick, and they're usually the last ones to be picked up! I was trying to set up an event, and Fred was early as always. He was taking things down as fast as I could set them up.

Now, in my prayer time, the Lord had given me the image of a fish, which I interpreted to mean the sign of a Christian which meant that I should get Fred into God's kingdom. Believe me, we had all been trying to no avail. So on this particular Sunday, I asked Fred, "Honey, do you like fish?"

He quickly responded, "I hate to eat fish, but I love to fish."

I asked, "Who takes you fishing?" Suddenly the truth dawned.

"Used to be my daddy, but since he left, I ain't been fishing."

Thank you, Lord!

"Would you like for me to find you someone to take you fishing?"

"Yes!"

So I did. A kind, retired man in our church led him to the fishing hole and to the Lord, and Fred is now a leader in our youth group. *Yes!* The love of God never fails!

M: Motivate. Children with A.D.D. seldom experience much success. They're likely to be off of their medication on the weekends, which makes it even more unlikely that the church will be a place for success. So we have to go the extra mile to help them succeed and feel welcome. Nothing motivates like success. Find something they can succeed in and then praise them.

N: Notes. Write notes of encouragement to kids with A.D.D. when they do well. Provide notes and checklists at strategic places such as by the backdoor, inside the car, inside a Bible, or inside a desk. They will fight you on your attempts to keep them organized, but they need it, so hang in there!

O: Oasis. Think of yourself as the **oasis of peace.** Gently redirect kids to a quiet activity, and help them get back on task without becoming more agitated. Children with A.D.D. often have *hypersensory* *acuity,* which means they are easily overstimulated. They need a hands-on, active-learning environment, but they also need breaks from that environment lest they become overstimulated. You, the adult, are the calm in their storm.

P: Praise. Praise works for everyone, but children with A.D.D. are especially starved for it.

Q: Quiet. Realize that kids with A.D.D. need quiet times as well. Make time in your lessons and places in your classroom where these kids can rest, reflect, and regroup.

R: Remind and Redirect. Yes, kids with A.D.D. need a few extras of these!

Think of it like this: If a child were hard of hearing or had a vision problem, you would happily accommodate him or her. These children have a behavior-regulator problem. Let's help them.

S: Step by step. Kids with A.D.D. need your help breaking things into doable steps. Remember, these kids think globally. It can be difficult for them to get from the parts to the whole. Show them the big picture first and then help them see how to take the first step.

T: Time-Out. Sometimes when you've tried everything, children with A.D.D. may still be spinning out in orbit. They may need to have a "cool-down space." This isn't necessarily a place for punishment, but rather a place to regroup. If you handle it correctly, these kids will welcome a time to rest.

U: Understanding. An understanding heart on the part of the adult can work wonders. It doesn't mean that we tolerate behavior that is wrong or ungodly. But we **understand** that when neurotransmitters are not fully operating in the behavior realm, training will take a little longer.

V: Victory. Victories will come in little steps. Celebrate them!

W: Welcome. Welcome kids with A.D.D. into your classroom. It may be the only place where they are truly welcomed. What better place for a child to be accepted and invited back than the house of the Lord!

X: Expectations can be enemies. When kids with A.D.D. are up against unrealistic expectations, it's hard on both the child and the teacher. You want to hold the standard high and expect the best, but be realistic and realize that there will be Sundays when you think you are going backward. Continue on. **Pray!** Persevere!

Y: You. God has chosen you to be in these children's lives and to love them. You may be the chosen ambassador to usher these children into God's kingdom. When you are having a bad day, consider the eternal focus of your work. Keep on keepin' on!

Z: Zeal. Your zeal for children, all God's children, even the hard-to-love, may reap eternal treasures you could never even begin to imagine. God doesn't make mistakes. All children are important to God, and he has a purpose for each one.

Need More Help?

For an in-depth discussion of A.D.D., its causes, diagnosis, treatment options, and reasons to **hope,** I'm happy to refer you to the many excellent references listed in the annotated bibliography.

Damaged Goods

Kids with A.D.D. are by no means the only ones who need an extra measure of love and understanding when they're in our classrooms. A lot of children are hurting today. The family unit is disintegrating. Many children are going through some aspect of the divorce process in which they have little or no "say-so." They feel powerless about losing the security of the family unit. These children tend to think it's their fault that their world is in pieces. They may not be given time to grieve or the help they need to heal following a divorce.

Many children come from homes where life is simply too hectic. There doesn't seem to be time for just *being* with one another as a family. There isn't time for talking quietly, playing games, snuggling, or reading books. Both parents may work. And no matter how much they'd like to give time to their children, they just can't make it happen. The day begins early and ends late, often with other caregivers filling in before and after school. Meals are grabbed at the fast-food drive-up window and gobbled down on the way to sporting events.

Children need *time*. The cliché is true: Love is spelled T-I-M-E. Often the greatest gifts you can give children in your classroom or in your home is to simply *stop* and *look* into their precious eyes. Listen to them. Talk to them. Connect with them. Give them *gifts of your time.*

Many of the same classroom strategies that help kids with A.D.D. also help kids who are hurried, harried, stressed, or suffer from other learning disabilities.

Ten Ways to Help Hurting Kids

1. Develop bridges of communication with these children. The time you take to develop relationships with these kids is in direct proportion to the decrease in time you'll have to spend in discipline situations with them.

2. Be an island of calm in their lives. Listen to them. Give warm, affirming eye contact and appropriate touch on necks, shoulders, or arms.

3. Be a bastion of fairness. Set clearly defined boundaries, and when they're violated, apply appropriate and immediate consequences. Then forgive, forget, and let the child start over with a clean slate.

4. Catch them doing something good! Be a mirror of their positive attitudes and behaviors. Let them know you believe in them.

5. Work on only one problem behavior at a time. Don't set up a chart for all thirty-two things they're doing wrong. Select the one behavior that is bugging you the most and help them conquer that. Praise their progress and then proceed to another behavior.

6. Be merciful by correcting them in private rather than in front of their peers. Take them to a corner of the classroom and have a quiet discussion about the problem behavior. Let them know that you understand and care about the difficult things in their lives. Before you let them go, affirm your confidence in them.

7. If a child is having a rough day, keep him or her physically close to you. "Rove" as you teach so you can intercept behavior problems and redirect kids to the task at hand.

8. Defuse difficult situations with gentle humor.

9. Let all the words that come out of your mouth be kind words. "Remember, the rule in our classroom is…" Avoid sarcasm and teasing that kids could misunderstand as put-downs.

10. Pray *for* kids and *with* them. When you feel your frustration level building, ask God to help you see these children through Jesus' eyes.

6 Teachers, Parents, and Their Partnership

Teacher Temperament Tendencies and Discipline

In my twenty-five years of working with teachers in public and private schools as well as in churches, I find that certain teacher temperament types offer particular challenges when it comes to discipline. Each teacher has unique gifts to bring to a teaching situation. We teach and discipline out of our personality and learning styles; this is who we are in the flesh. When we are reborn in Jesus Christ, our natural tendencies are refined as we grow in spiritual maturity and receive our spiritual gifts from the Holy Spirit to be used in ministry. Our ultimate goal is to grow to be like Jesus, the master teacher.

Regardless of our personalities, learning styles, or spiritual gifts, we may have to do a *paradigm shift.* A *paradigm* is roughly equivalent to tradition. The word not only refers to how we do things, but more accurately, it refers to how we explain or understand a part of reality. When we undergo a *paradigm shift,* we find a new way to interpret the facts or a creative way to approach a dilemma. In nearly every field, the truly significant advances are made when people break with the traditional way of thinking. Perhaps it's time for children's workers in the church to make a paradigm shift in how we handle discipline.

To do that, it's helpful to take a look at ourselves as teachers and understand what we bring to the classroom and what our natural strengths are as well as some of the challenges we're likely to face. The D teacher—we'll call him Mr. D. Manding—is the one likely to say: "Those boys need someone to teach them who's boss. What they need is discipline!" The I teacher, Miss I. M. Inspiring, loves all of God's children. Sometimes she just can't bear to discipline the children because they are such "precious little lambs." Mr. S. Tatus Quo, the S teacher, wants peace at any cost. Because he's so easygoing, he may miss classroom problems that need to be addressed. On the other hand, Mr. Dewit Wright, the C teacher, reads books on discipline, meticulously prepares each lesson, and has an ideal vision of how class should be. Mr. Wright has difficulty handling the unplanned episodes of childishness that inevitably happen in any class.

Let's take a look at the four different temperaments from the DiSC® model and discover how teachers of each temperament are likely to relate to children of different temperaments. Once again, we've assigned a specific male or female nickname for the sake of discussion, but people of both genders can fall into any of the four categories.

Mr. D. Manding Teacher Profile:

Temperament—He is a D (dynamic, demanding) on the DiSC model. Mr. D. Manding is task-oriented and outgoing.

Scripture to Live By—*Without leadership a nation falls, but lots of good advice will save it (Proverbs 11:14).*

Biblical Example—Paul

Characteristics—
- a born leader
- take-charge
- impatient
- stimulates activity
- dynamic
- organizes well
- finds it hard to apologize
- doer

Mr. D. Manding's Disciplinary Style

✓ He has no trouble providing discipline; in fact, he thrives on it. This teacher may have to learn how to soften his approach.

✓ His organizational skills make the discipline clear to follow.

✓ With his tendency to be impatient and his difficulty admitting that he's wrong, he may overpower some of his students. For students who like challenge and competition, this may work. But for his more sensitive students, he may have to temper his natural tendencies with compassion.

Challenges for Mr. D. Manding:

✓ to realize that not everyone is as motivated to activity as he is.
✓ to be sensitive to other people's feelings.
✓ to learn to apologize.
✓ to let children be who they are and not try to control them.

Here's a simplified look at how a teacher similar to Mr. D. Manding might relate to kids of different temperaments.

Dynamic Dan	Inspiring Ingrid	Steady Steve	Conscientious Connie
Watch out for Fourth of July fireworks as the two wills collide. Both the student and the teacher may create confrontations and standoffs as both remain determined to win.	The teacher dominates; the student feels unloved. She may try harder to please the teacher, but she doesn't understand *why* a change is needed, so she may not learn the value of new behaviors. She comes into class as fresh as a daisy and may leave as a wilted flower.	Again, the teacher overcomes, and the student appears compliant. But the student may "stuff" deep resentment. The real goal of discipline—an inward change in behavior—may not be realized.	The teacher may overwhelm this student. Without encouragement, this child slowly dries up and withers on the vine. This child is a perfectionist who wants to do things right, but feels that she can never live up to the demands of the teacher.

Miss I. M. Inspiring Teacher Profile:

Temperament—She is an I (influencing, inspiring) on the DiSC® model. This teacher is an extrovert who loves to have fun!

Scripture to Live By—*Worry is a heavy load, but a kind word cheers you up (Proverbs 12:25).*

Biblical Example—Peter

Characteristics—
- fun-loving
- loves a stage
- forgetful
- spontaneous
- an appealing personality
- energetic
- a good sense of humor
- will apologize
- not good with details (lesson plans, schedules)

Miss I. M. Inspiring's Disciplinary Style
✓ Because of her "up" disposition and her creativity, her class will be lively and fun and kids will be less likely to act out.

✓ She will want to focus on the fun part of teaching and avoid nitty-gritty discipline issues.

✓ Her love of being "on stage" and entertaining her students may make it difficult for her to get students to "switch gears" to more serious matters.

Challenges for Miss I. M. Inspiring:

✓ to define rules and boundaries of appropriate behavior and to write and post those rules.

✓ to work toward being consistent in her approach to discipline, rather than always spontaneous.

✓ to accept the fact that even though consistent discipline isn't fun, it's a necessary and important part of her job.

Here's a simplified look at how a teacher similar to Miss I. M. Inspiring might relate to kids of different temperaments.

Dynamic Dan	Inspiring Ingrid	Steady Steve	Conscientious Connie
The student may win unless the teacher is willing to back up her discipline with "tough love."	The student and the teacher may become too "buddy-buddy" and forget the order of things.	This relationship works only because the student is so easy to manage.	These two don't relate well. The student thinks the teacher is too frivolous. The teacher may forget to be an adult and remain in charge.

Mr. S. Tatus Quo Teacher Profile:

Temperament—He is an S (steady, status quo) on the DiSC® model. Mr. S. Tatus Quo is an introverted, easygoing people-person.

Scripture to Live By—*A gentle answer will calm a person's anger, but an unkind answer will cause more anger (Proverbs 15:1).*

Biblical Example—Abraham

Characteristics—
- patient
- quiet
- balanced
- good interior organization
- happy, reconciled to life
- can be stubborn or lazy
- a peacemaker
- calm
- fair

Mr. S. Tatus Quo's Disciplinary Style

✓ He has the potential to be the best at discipline because of his great sense of internal organization.

✓ He has great patience with kids.

✓ Because of his gentle, easygoing nature, students will tend to cooperate with him.

✓ This person's natural ability to "hold it together" even during stressful times makes him able to be a fair disciplinarian.

✓ Because he's a patient peacemaker, he remains rational when challenged and doesn't overreact emotionally.

Challenges for Mr. S. Tatus Quo:

✓ to overcome his natural tendency to be lax in discipline.

✓ to define a system for discipline and stick to it. His easygoing nature tends to allow him to let things slide by.

✓ To maintain the perspective that discipline is a necessary part of "tough love."

Here's a simplified look at how a teacher similar to Mr. S. Tatus Quo might relate to kids of different temperaments.

Dynamic Dan	**I**nspiring Ingrid	**S**teady Steve	**C**onscientious Connie
The student may dominate because the teacher is so easygoing. The teacher needs to have a plan to ward off the student's attempt to gain control.	This student tends to be forgetful and silly, and the teacher doesn't remind her of the rules because he doesn't want to rock the boat.	The teacher will enjoy this student because he is a bastion of order and peace in a lively, somewhat chaotic classroom.	The student craves an environment that is "right"; if the teacher allows other students to be out of control, this student will be very unhappy.

Mr. Dewit Wright Teacher Profile:

Temperament—He is a C (conscientious, cautious) on the DiSC® model. The motto of this teacher is his name: Dewit Wright! (or "Do it right!")

Scripture to Live By—*Those who get wisdom do themselves a favor, and those who love learning will succeed (Proverbs 19:8).*

Biblical Example—Moses

Characteristics—
- organized
- compassionate
- conscientious
- perfectionistic
- devoted
- may be rigid
- may be hard to please because of high standards

Mr. Dewit Wright's Disciplinary Style

✓ Because his classroom is well-organized and his lessons well-prepared, he will have fewer discipline problems than more easygoing teachers.

✓ Because he wants to do everything right, he will be tenacious about learning effective ways to discipline.

✓ Because he's perfectionistic and hard to please, some children may act out because they feel inadequate to meet his high expectations.

Challenges for Mr. Wright:

✓ to lower his expectations and accept students who are willing to settle for doing less than their best.

✓ to "lighten up" in his approach to discipline.

✓ to be positive and less critical of children.

Here's a simplified look at how a teacher similar to Mr. Wright might relate to kids of different temperaments.

Dynamic Dan	Inspiring Ingrid	Steady Steve	Conscientious Connie
This student wants control and may take this teacher right to the wall. The teacher must stand firm but delegate some control and some choices to the student within the clearly defined parameters of the teacher's authority.	The teacher's insistence on doing things right may get on the nerves of this student. The student may be heard to mutter under her breath, "Chill out."	It works because the student is organized and quiet. The teacher appreciates the student's calming influence and his efforts as a peacemaker.	This relationship works because both want the same sense of ideal order and justice. Problems may develop if both get stuck on an issue at the same time. If "paralysis of analysis" hits both, they could sink into emotional quicksand.

Learning Styles and Teacher Tendencies

As a general rule, teaching tends to attract people who are logical, organized, and orderly. **Organizers** like things to be neat and predictable. In fact, when these teachers were children, they probably did not misbehave much at all. That makes it difficult for them to understand and accept children who operate outside the neat and tidy zone of the organizer. While organizers make excellent disciplinarians and teachers, they often have to work at accepting children who don't fall within their narrow criteria of acceptable behavior. This poses some interesting discipline challenges.

If this paragraph describes you,
- thank God for your organizational skills, but
- recognize the wonderful (though very different) qualities of children who are completely spontaneous and disorganized; and
- remember that God "wired" each of us differently and that there's no one "right" way to operate.

In math and science careers, you'll find a fair number of people who are **Researchers.** They enjoy the world of theory, logic, research, and analysis. What are they like as teachers? They may be aloof and a bit absent-minded. They're so fascinated by the intellectual world that they may have trouble relating to the everyday world of children.

This person has to read, research, study, and think through a clear system of discipline. Researchers may have to deal with the frustration that comes from the fact that children are unpredictable. Their neat theories about what kids will do don't play out in the classroom. If this paragraph describes you,
- work at connecting with kids on the feeling level, and
- work toward spontaneity.

Teachers who are **Relaters** are very loving people who think with their hearts. They're affectionate with kids and seem to relate well to children of many different temperaments. They tend to believe that if they simply love a child enough, he or she will behave. If this paragraph describes you,
- enjoy the warm relationships you have with kids, and
- learn to use "tough love" when it's appropriate; otherwise kids may take advantage of you.

Doers who work in the multiple-task mode are strong-willed and have probably tried most everything themselves that a similarly wired child will try on them! These people usually do a great job with discipline because they can intuitively second-guess strong-willed children. These teachers tend to be creative and fun. If this paragraph describes you,

- rejoice in your creativity, and
- be careful of overwhelming children who are more reserved.

For each kind of teacher temperament, there are inherent strengths and weaknesses. Let us remember that each of us is a unique combination of temperament traits, spiritual gifts, and other qualities. When our particular combination of traits comes up against another set of unique temperament traits, the response is one of a kind. The simplified interaction charts given in the teacher temperament section offer just the merest clue as to what kinds of relationships might result when teachers of certain temperaments work with children of other temperaments.

In these relationships, the adult is nearly always in the position of power. As kids enter adolescence, the power pendulum may swing back and forth, but for the most part, the adult retains control. That's why it's so important that we know ourselves, that we understand our strengths in working with kids, and that we're aware of our weaknesses.

Parenting Preferences

In many cases, teaching and parenting tendencies may be quite similar: temperament-related discipline issues may carry over into both realms. Here's a quick look at how parents and children of different temperaments may interact.

Mr. D. Manding's Parenting Preferences

Dynamic Dan	**I**nspiring Ingrid	**S**teady Steve	**C**onscientious Connie
Look for a collision of wills. The parent will try to control the relationship at any cost.	The parent will probably tend to hurt the child's feelings. The child may feel unloved because it's hard for Mr. D. Manding to express affection.	The relationship may appear OK on the surface, but the child may hide inner feelings of resentment.	The parent may overwhelm the child. Though she tries hard to please, the child may not feel unconditional love.

Miss I. M. Inspiring's Parenting Preferences

Dynamic Dan	Inspiring Ingrid	Steady Steve	Conscientious Connie
The parent may have a hard time disciplining this child because it's not fun! The child may not take the parent seriously.	The parent and the child will enjoy a fun and spontaneous relationship. They may forget who is the parent and who is the child.	The parent and the child will share a comfortable, easygoing relationship. Both are "people-persons" who will enjoy being together.	The child may think the parent is too frivolous. The parent and child may not relate well. The child may feel some role reversal with the adult.

Mr. S. Tatus Quo's Parenting Preferences

Dynamic Dan	Inspiring Ingrid	Steady Steve	Conscientious Connie
The parent may have trouble managing this child. The child may try to wrestle control from the adult.	The parent and child will probably enjoy a relaxed, happy relationship.	Both parent and child will be comfortable in a warm, accepting relationship. They will enjoy each other.	The parent may not relate to the moodiness of the child. The parent can successfully discipline this child.

Mr. Dewit Wright's Parenting Preferences

Dynamic Dan	Inspiring Ingrid	Steady Steve	Conscientious Connie
The parent may be overwhelmed dealing with this child and feel depressed about his lack of success in discipline.	The parent and child may find it difficult to relate to each other. The parent's expectations may be too high.	This will be an easy, enjoyable relationship. The child will make the parent look good.	This parent and child will understand each other. They need to guard against becoming overly sensitive with each other.

Teachers and Parents as Partners

Parents and teachers in the church share a unique partnership in teaching children to know, love, and follow Jesus. At a time in our country when education was at its peak, it was understood that the primary responsibility for raising children belonged to the parents. Delegated authority went to the church. Today, we have delegated part of the responsibility of raising our children to the government, and in so doing, we have weakened our family unit and ultimately society at large.

Parents need help today more than ever. Our society grows more complex and lifestyles more hectic. With both parents working and stretched to the limit and with so many single parents doing their very best to keep households together, families are hurried, harried, and just hanging on. As a church, we can play an important role in coming alongside parents and helping them raise their children in the ways of God.

Children are like mirrors; their behavior is a reflection of the whirl of life around them. The message children are sending to us is that we live in a world gone crazy. If we want to get discipline back under control, we need to slow the world down for our children. Society shows no sign of slowing down—but rather seems to be growing more chaotic. The only times of rest and quiet our children will know is what we provide them in our homes and in our churches.

As teachers in the church, we can impress upon parents and children the importance of turning off the television, telephones, fax machines, and computers. We can encourage families to read together, to talk, and to play games. Parents have precious few hours to give to their children, and those hours must be invested wisely. Teachers in the church have just an hour a week to pass on the wonderful truths in God's holy Word. Let us join together to hold our children close and to teach them the joys of discipleship.

It is important that we, as Christian educators, find ways to walk hand in hand with the parents in the raising of their children. Parental involvement is the secret to high educational success with children. Find ways for parents to be involved in the programs at your church. On a periodic basis, send home forms that show different levels of involvement such as teaching, assisting in classes, working as game- or craft-leaders, providing help with bulletin boards, or organizing social activities.

It's important for teachers to know the parents of their students by name and to develop relationships with them. If parents deliver a child to the door, introduce yourself and begin to form a friendship. Send home simple notes about what's happening in the class and about the child's progress. We don't want to fall into the habit of only speaking with parents when there's bad news to be delivered!

Occasionally you will need to talk to a parent about a child's behavior in class. It's wise to approach parents discreetly and in private. If you march down the hall to find a parent, dragging the child by the ear, the parent will not be happy to see you. If you come "on offense," a parent has no recourse but to defend. Announcing in front of onlookers that you need a conference will also put parents on the defensive. Help the parent to maintain some dignity in the situation. Position yourself as a helpful support person.

The Sweeten-It-Up Sandwich

When you need to talk with a parent about a child's behavior, always begin with something positive. If you find it hard to think of something positive to say about the child, pray about it. God *will* reveal something positive for you to say. After your positive statement, put this statement in the middle of the sandwich: "But I am having a little problem with (child's name), and I was wondering if you could help me." That statement makes the problem yours—it's much easier for parents to digest than, "*Your* child is *very* disruptive in my classroom, and I need you to stop him *now.*" Whew! No parent wants to hear those words.

When you gently state a problem and take ownership of it, the parent has time to think. True, you may be having a *major* problem, and you may feel like throttling the child, but a gentle answer turns away the wrath of the parent. Chances are, if you're having problems with this student at church, the student is probably having problems at school, too. The parents may be thinking, "Oh, no—here we go again."

Encourage the parent to share discipline mechanisms that work well with the child at home or at school. Listen carefully, and ask questions to clarify. Most parents respond well to a teacher asking for their help and will be willing to share what they've learned that "works" with their child. Sometimes this leads to parents sharing their own frustrations and opens a door for ministry to the whole family.

Then it's time to put the lid on the sandwich—another positive statement about the child and a plan of action that both parties have agreed upon.

If a second contact is needed, I often involve the child. This sends an important message to the child: "We all care for you and are working together toward a positive solution to help you." It communicates a team effort instead of setting up an "us against them" scenario. State the problem and then turn to the child and ask, "Is that how you see it?" This approach helps the child take ownership of the problem. It also prevents the child from later claiming, "That's not what really happened."

If problems continue, you may want to ask the parent to come to class and sit with the child. One or two sessions with Mom or Dad in the class often works wonders for the child.

This technique worked well with a child who was a constant distraction in a second-grade Sunday school classroom. Having his mother sit with him in class made no difference—he may as well have come to class alone. However, when Dad came with him, he was a changed boy. Further talks with the parents revealed that Dad worked out of town all week and was only home for part of Saturday and Sunday. The child was starved for Dad's attention! Unfortunately, the father was not able to change his work schedule, but he did learn how important it was for him to spend as much time as possible with his son. In this instance, placing the boy with a male teacher helped his behavior at church.

Parent-Teacher Temperaments

Because the positive interaction of parents and teachers is so important, let's look at how various parent-teacher behavioral combinations might work. The interesting twist to this setup is that when two parents are involved, they are very likely to have opposite temperaments. (Most of us do marry our opposites, which is part of God's great character-building school!)

The goal of a parent-teacher partnership is to create a bridge of understanding to help a child. When personalities clash, however, the bridge can turn into a roadblock! How can we prevent this from happening? The two differing personalities need to learn to relate to one another, receive what each other is communicating, and reinforce each other's strengths in order to help the child.

These charts based on the DiSC® model offer insights into how parents and teachers can relate to each other, receive what each other is saying, and reinforce each other's strengths.

Dominant, Demanding Temperament

How to respond to a D:	How to relate to a D:	How to reinforce a D:
Be firm and direct, and focus on the student's actions.	Be brief and to the point. Use logic to develop a plan to help the student.	Repeat the plan and give bottom-line goals, objectives, and a timetable.

Influencing, Inspiring Temperament

How to respond to an I:	How to relate to an I:	How to reinforce an I:
Be friendly and positive, and allow time for interaction.	Let them talk about their feelings and then transfer them to a plan of action to help the child.	Offer positive encouragement and incentives for solving this discipline problem.

Steady, Status Quo Temperament

How to respond to an S:	How to relate to an S:	How to reinforce an S:
Be nonthreatening and patient, and allow time for them to process the information.	Use personal acceptance and assurance, and gently discuss ways to solve the problem.	Be patient in allowing them to take ownership of the idea and partner with you in dealing with it.

Conscientious, Cautious Temperament

How to respond to a C:	How to relate to a C:	How to reinforce a C:
Make allowances for initial responses to be cautious or negative.	Discuss the situation in a logical, persistent manner.	Provide a step-by-step approach for reaching the goal; provide assurances of support.

Tips for Talking to Teachers

● Remember how difficult the teacher's job is. Teachers deal with your child *and* a room full of other children. Remember how frustrated you can feel some days just dealing with your own child. Enter the conversation with empathy.

● Pray for a teachable spirit. Pray for the Lord to give you ears to hear the truth and the grace to forgive and forget what may be simply venting on the part of the teacher.

● Remember that each of us is "wired" differently. Some children have the ability to take a teacher to the wall quickly. Be aware of the teacher's fatigue and frustration.

● Don't grab a teacher before or after class. Set up an appointment. Come in with a friendly attitude. In fact, you might even bring a plate of goodies.

● Start with a positive statement of appreciation for all the teacher is doing. Highlight something your child likes about the class. Then gently state: "I wonder if you've had any problems with my child. What can I do to help?" This opens the door for discussion without making the teacher feel defensive.

● Close with a positive statement and readiness to implement a positive plan of action. Children can always sense when parents and teachers are walking "hand in hand." In the long run, it is much better for your child when he or she sees you and the teacher cooperating with each other.

Put Yourself in This Picture

Let's take a look at a possible parent-teacher interaction and try two different response patterns.

The teacher has had a challenging Sunday morning. She woke up with a headache, and she had had a hard week at work and didn't get the time she wanted to prepare the lesson. On top of that, she was up with a sick child during the night. The teacher for the second hour did not show up, so she had to teach both hours. Your child was the first to arrive in the morning and now is the last to be picked up. It is storming outside, and your child has created a similar storm in the classroom with his erratic behavior. It's been a tough Sunday.

You, the parent, sing in the choir and had to get there early. So you deposited your child in the classroom where he would be supervised. You were late picking up your child and then stopped to visit with a friend. Now you're heading down the hallway to your child's classroom. You can hear the teacher saying: "Where in the world is your mother? Doesn't she know that Sunday school got out twenty minutes ago? Now stop taking those pictures off the bulletin board! How many times have I told you…" You feel anger building up inside as you stand in the door. *How **dare** she talk to **your** child that way?* Then you become the target of her frustration.

The teacher sees you, looks at her watch, and asks: "Didn't you realize that class got out twenty minutes ago? All the other children have been picked up. Alan has been impossible all morning. He tore up my display. He won't listen. He hit three children. Don't you ever discipline this child?"

What is your response? (If you, the parent, respond with equal fury, the situation will escalate.) You defensively grab your child and exit, muttering unkind remarks about the teacher. The more you think about it, the more angry you become. What kinds of consequences does the child receive for this? You may take out your anger on your child and spank him when you get home, or you may be a "Mamma Bear" and overprotect your child from this "mean ol' teacher who doesn't understand you, sweetheart." In either case, the child does not learn appropriate consequences for his actions. Everyone is angry, and no progress has been made to avoid a second scene like this one.

A more effective response from the teacher:

● Don't blame the child for the parent bringing him early and leaving him late.

● As you wait for the parent, spend valuable one-on-one time with the child.

● Greet the parent with a positive statement.

● Take ownership of the problems. "I've been having a problem with Alan's behavior today. Do you have any ideas how I might keep him happily occupied? I wonder if there's a way we can arrange for Alan to receive care before and after class on days when he needs to come early and stay after others have left."

● Close with a positive statement and a plan of action. "Thanks for your tip of setting out Legos for Alan to play with as I set up and clean up the room. Let's ask the Education Committee if they can address the needs of children whose parents come early for choir practice."

A more effective response from the parent:

● Don't go on the defensive; understand the teacher's point of view.

● Hear the teacher's concerns with a gentle spirit.

● Try to be part of the solution. The words, "What can I do to help?" are a healing balm.

● Offer your child a choice of reasonable consequences for his behavior.

● Smile and go on.

The Common Goal

Discipline is training a child in mind, body, and character to enable him or her to become a self-controlled, constructive member of society. Discipline requires training through a variety of means such as moral guidance, example, verbal instructions, written plan, and an agenda of realistic expectations. Discipline is much easier when children receive plenty of time and attention from parents and teachers and truly feel loved and appreciated for who and what they are.

Handling discipline effectively is a hallmark of a successful teacher or parent. Yet this area is one which causes the most burnout and fatigue in both parents and teachers. Why? Probably because it is so ongoing. Also, children are becoming more difficult to manage because of the influence of society. There seems to be a total lack of respect for authority that is permeating our culture; the media reflects this position to our children, and they reflect it back to us.

But a wake-up call is resounding through our nation. Educators and parents are looking at what is happening to our children today and seeking ways to improve the situation. What will it take? A committed joining of forces between parents and churches. We need to look at the incredible impact that the media is having on our kids. The statistics are alarming. If you want to take a deeper look at this issue, may I suggest you read *Right From Wrong* by Josh McDowell and Bob Hostetler (Word Publishing) and *Learn to Discern* by Robert G. DeMoss, Jr. (Zondervan Publishing House).

We must bring godly discipline back into our homes, schools, and churches. We must not run away from this issue but instead tackle it straight on. We need to start spending more time with our children instead of rushing them from one program to another. We must turn off the television and learn to talk and interact with one another again. We must pray to see our children as God designed them to be.

Discipline is a discipling process. We provide external guidance that trains children to learn to apply internal guidance. It's a process that takes time. Let's give kids our time—they need it. Let's show our love for kids as we patiently and persistently discipline them to the glory of God.

7 Get It Together!

Understanding that discipline is a discipling process and that our goal is to be mentors who help children learn to know, love, and follow Jesus, how do we begin to put this knowledge to work in our churches? And how can we share these ideas with other children's workers to bring them "on board?"

This chapter offers you two active-learning training sessions for the children's workers in your church. The goal of these sessions is to set discipline guidelines that you'll use across the board in your children's programs—guidelines that administrators, teachers, helpers, and kids can all live with. You'll find step-by-step instructions for each training session as well as photocopiable handouts with all the tools and information your teachers will need to get up and rolling with positive discipline in every classroom.

One of the best things you'll ever do for the kids in your church is to establish unified discipline policies and procedures—policies that are understood and implemented by every teacher in every classroom. In Chapter 1, we covered the three major reasons kids misbehave: ignorance of the rules, conflicting rules, and frustration. When each teacher sets his or her own rules, kids get confused about which rules apply in which settings. A unified discipline policy offers kids—and teachers—the security of knowing exactly what is expected of them, whether it's in Sunday school, at children's choir, or in a midweek program.

Working together to create a unified discipline policy gives teachers and helpers confidence that they can appropriately handle any situation that comes up. As they work through these training sessions together, teachers will learn to understand and embrace the philosophy behind each rule and guideline they agree upon. This foundational understanding is critical to honest, loving, and appropriate application of the discipline program.

Training Session 1
Loving Your Kids to Good Behavior

1. The Power of Sweet-and-Sour

You'll need photocopies of the "Discipline Training: Session One Outline" handout (p. 148), pencils, and sour-ball candies that are sweet on the inside.

Ask all participants to stand up. Then ask those who have no discipline problems in their classrooms to sit down. (Few, if any, will sit.)

Say: **Look around! If you're having some discipline problems in your classroom, you're not alone. Discipline is a troublesome area for even the most experienced teachers. Recent Gallup polls have found that the general public sees classroom discipline as the number one problem in American education.**

Before you sit down, think back to your own childhood. Think what it felt like to be a child in a classroom. Share with the group a time when you misbehaved—it could be a specific instance of misbehavior, or it could be a situation in which you typically got in trouble. After you've shared, you may sit down.

If some participants are already sitting down, invite them to share a time from their childhoods when it was difficult for them to "behave."

Give each participant a sweet-and-sour candy. Let them eat their way to the sweet part and then have them form pairs and discuss these questions with their partners.

● **How was eating this candy like disciplining kids? How was it different?** (It wasn't pleasant at first, but later it got better; it took patience to get to the sweet part; getting to the sweet part made it worth going through the sour part.)

● **How was eating this candy like or unlike being disciplined? How was it different?** (It hurt my mouth and then it got sweet; kids don't like it at first, but eventually they realize that it's worth it.)

Allow several people to share their responses with the whole group. Then distribute pencils and the "Discipline Training: Session One Outline" handouts (p. 148). Read aloud Hebrews 12:11 from the top of the outline.

Say: **Discipline is a mixed bag for both kids and teachers.** Ask the following questions, pausing after each question to allow several people to respond. Ask:

● **How would you define discipline?**
● **What's the purpose of discipline?**
● **What do you think the goal of classroom discipline in our church should be?**

Then say: **Discipline is more than controlling a child. It is a balance of unconditional love and straightforward guidance lovingly combined in the long-term process of nurturing a child into maturity. Many kids and adults confuse discipline and punishment. Punishment involves shame and blame. That's not what we're about. Yes, there must be consequences for wrong behavior, but that's just one small part of the process. The word "discipline" (which makes kids cringe) comes from the word "disciple." We can all feel good about helping kids become disciples of Jesus.** Ask:

- **What's involved in being a disciple?**
- **What's involved in making disciples?**

Say: **The first thing we need to understand as we work toward creating a unified discipline program for our church is that we're not focusing on punishment—we're focusing on making disciples of Jesus Christ.**

2. Understanding Behavior Problems

You'll need a dry-erase board or a pad of newsprint, a marker, and a noisemaker.

Say: **Maybe things haven't changed so much over the years! Let's take a closer look and see if we can understand the problem behaviors we see in our classrooms.**

Have participants form groups of four. Ask each group to assign these roles: a Facilitator (the person with the most children at home) who will keep the group on track; a Recorder (the teacher with the most experience) who will write down the group's ideas; a Reporter (the newest teacher) who will share the ideas with the whole group; and a Cheerleader (the remaining person) who encourages everyone to participate.

Say: **Many of you told about times when you misbehaved as a child. Now I'd like you to tell each other *why* you misbehaved! I'd like to hear from several of you.** After several people have shared, say: **Now I'd like you to take three minutes to brainstorm reasons that kids misbehave today. Reporters, please jot down the reasons for misbehavior that your group brainstorms. Go.** Give a one-minute warning and then use the noisemaker to call time. Ask the Reporters to share their groups' ideas.

Say: **I have a very short list of reasons children misbehave. Let's see if your reasons and mine match up.** Write these headings on a dry-erase board or newsprint: Ignorance of the Rules, Conflicting Rules, and Frustration. Let participants comment on how their ideas might fall under each of the headings.

Then say: **If we want to eliminate discipline problems, we need to begin by eliminating the reasons for them. Let's begin with "Ignorance of the Rules."** Ask:

● **How can we make certain that kids know and understand our rules for conduct in our church's programs?**

Say: **It's not fair to kids if we just assume that they know what our expectations are. Rules need to be spelled out regularly in class, and the consequences need to be stated clearly and applied consistently. Begin each new class with a discussion of your expectations and then repeat the expectations about every month or as you see your class starting to forget them.** Ask:

● **Why do you think our kids are sometimes confused by conflicting rules?**

Say: **Our students come from a variety of home situations. Each family has different expectations for their kids. Sunday school teachers may have slightly different expectations in their classrooms. Kids who attend preschool or elementary school may be presented with yet another set of expectations. What's acceptable in one place may be unacceptable in another. Part of our goal is to create a unified discipline plan that we'll implement in all our children's programs. Then we'll all know what to expect, and so will the kids we teach.**

Write the heading "What Causes Frustration?" on a dry-erase board or newsprint. Ask:

● **Why do you think children sometimes get frustrated in our classes?**

List responses. Summarize by saying: **Many things can cause frustration for kids. Not all of them have to do with the teacher, but most of them connect to the teacher in one way or another.** If participants haven't already mentioned these reasons for frustration, add them to your list.

● boredom—the lesson seems uninteresting, irrelevant, or a repetition of "the same old thing"
● other kids who act out, if the teacher fails to make them behave
● failure—the activities in the lesson aren't age-appropriate
● stories or activities that are too long for a child's attention span
● distractions inside and outside the class
● constantly being reprimanded

3. Learn From the Master Teacher

You'll need Bibles.

Say: **I'd like you to think back to your childhood once again. This time, see if you can recall a punishment or consequence** that made you really angry. Ask:

● **Who can tell about a punishment that made you feel like the world was unfair?** (You might suggest punishments such as being sent to bed without dinner, being yelled at in front of peers, or having to write a word or sentence several times.)

● **Why did that punishment make you so angry?**

Say: **Punishment involves shaming, blaming, and paying back. Discipline involves helping children see what was wrong with their actions, making sure they understand how to do better next time, and allowing them to pay the natural consequences of what they did wrong. We don't want to do things in our classrooms that kids will remember years later because they felt shamed or punished unfairly.**

In teacher-student relationships, the adult is almost always in a position of power. The teacher controls almost everything about the condition of the classroom (except the physical structure itself), including the atmosphere and mood, the comfort level, the preparedness or lack of it, and the style of discipline.

So it's important for us to know and use the best approach to discipline. And that's probably simpler than you might imagine: We need to require ourselves to understand the needs of kids and prepare ourselves to meet those needs appropriately. When we apply ourselves to accomplishing those ends, we'll stop most behavior problems before they get started! Above all, we need always to bear in mind that our students are children of God who deserve to be treated with respect and dignity.

Let's take a look at Jesus' attitude toward children and his interaction with them. Have volunteers read aloud Matthew 18:1-5 and 19:13-15. Ask:

● **What was Jesus' attitude toward children?**

● **Why do you think Jesus held up children as examples and role models?**

● **Why did Jesus' disciples have such a different view of children?**

● **In our interaction with children at church, are we more like Jesus or more like his disciples? Explain.**

● **What do we need to do to be more Christlike as we deal with children?**

Say: **Think of one, two, or three children you deal with in your class or ministry—kids who try your patience or are difficult to like. Draw stick figures on the back of your outline to represent those children.** Pause as participants draw.

Say: **Please place your papers on your open palms as we**

sing "Jesus Loves the Little Children."

Lead the group in singing the chorus and then say: **Jesus loved and respected children, even when he was overwhelmed with people demanding his attention. Jesus made time for children when it would have been easier for him to push them aside and deal with more "important" adult issues. If Jesus respected children this much, shouldn't we as teachers have that same sort of respect? In fact, respecting children is the first step toward having a positive classroom and minimizing discipline challenges.**

You've shown just by being here in this training session that you're willing to take time for children and that you're willing to respect and understand them. Let's take a few moments to look at kids' basic needs and discover some practical ways we can meet those needs in our classrooms.

4. Kids' Needs and How to Meet Them

You'll need photocopies of the "Safe, Appropriate Touch" handout (p. 147). Cut the handouts into three parts, and place the three parts in three separate corners of the room.

Say: **In his book *Understanding People*, Larry Crabb tells us what children need in order to be at their best. Listen as I read a brief excerpt from his book.**

> Children, I suspect, would become more manageable and infinitely more lovable if parents [or teachers, (our addition)] would answer, properly and with some consistency, a few elementary questions that all kids ask. First, "Am I loved?" Correct answer: "Yes, deeply—and here's the unmistakable evidence of my rich, committed involvement with you." Second, "Can I get my own way?" Correct answer: "No, not without cost—and here is a sample of the painful consequences that result from bucking against God's plan."

Ask:

● **What did you learn from that passage that you can apply in your ministry to kids?**

Say: **Children behave better when their emotional needs are consistently met; we've all seen children demonstrate this. When kids are emotionally distraught, they simply don't cope with life as well. When kids are happy and their emotional needs are satisfied, they deal with frustrations, waiting, and** pretty much everything else just a little bit better.

Ross Campbell, a pediatric psychologist, tells us the three essentials for communicating love to a child: pleasant, meaningful eye contact; appropriate physical affection; and focused attention. **Let's see how we can meet these needs of children in our classrooms.**

Everyone with birthdays that fall in the months between January and June, please stand up. Now position yourselves beside someone who's still sitting down. It's OK if there's more than one person standing by a sitting person. Standing people, without moving anything but your mouths, tell the person you're standing beside that he or she is one of the nicest people you know. Pause as participants do this.

Then say: **Now I'd like the January to June birthday people to sit down and the July to December people to stand up. July to December people, please get comfortably close to the people you're standing beside and give them pleasant eye contact as you say, "You're one of the nicest people I know."**

Pause as participants do this. Then direct everyone to sit down. Ask:

● **What was the difference between those two experiences?**

● **How do you think the eye-contact comfort zone changes as kids get older?**

Say: **In order to communicate our love and acceptance to kids, we need to look them in the eyes as we speak to them. Let's move on to giving kids appropriate physical affection. This is a difficult issue today. There are some important guidelines and safeguards that children's workers need to know and practice. Let's learn them. The first is to have two adults in a room, or one adult and one teenager. This allows one person to vouch for the other.**

The second guideline is to touch children in ways that won't be misinterpreted as suggestive. To learn how to do that, form trios. In your trios, decide who will be a One, a Two, and a Three.

Send the Ones to one corner, the Twos to another corner, and the Threes to the third corner. Say: **Everyone should pick up a handout in your corner. Choose one person in each corner to read the handout aloud. Once you've read the handouts and practiced what's written on them, return to your trios. Teach what you've learned to the other members of your trio.**

Allow time for trios to interact. Give a one-minute warning and then call time. Gather everyone in a circle, and say: **The third way** to communicate love is to give kids focused attention. Ask:

● **When are times you can talk one-on-one with your students?**

Say: **We've learned important concepts today that will form the foundation of our unified discipline program which we'll put together in our next meeting.**

Be sure everyone is aware of the time and location of your next meeting. Encourage everyone to bring the "Discipline Training: Session One Outline" (p. 148) to the next meeting. Close with prayer, thanking God for the privilege of discipling his children.

Safe, Appropriate Touch

Group 1: The Scruff Squeeze

With children of any age, it's important that affection appear and be received as an innocent gesture. "Bony" parts of the body, such as the neck, shoulder, or hand, tend to be "safe zones." Practice giving each other quick squeezes on the neck, hand, or shoulder as you say, "I'm so glad you're here today." Then return to your trios to share and demonstrate what you've learned.

Group 2: Hit and Run

Affirming physical contact with students is best given quickly rather than with a lingering touch. Practice giving each other quick, affirming touches as you say, "Way to go!" Then return to your trios to share and demonstrate what you've learned.

Group 3: The Open-Faced Sandwich

It will help you avoid misunderstandings and accusations if you will remember to touch "out in the open." An open position (side by side) is preferable to a closed one (front to front). Practice giving each other "open" affirming touches as you say, "Good job!" Then return to your trios to share and demonstrate what you've learned.

Discipline Training: Session One Outline

We do not enjoy being disciplined. It is painful, but later, after we have learned from it, we have peace, because we start living in the right way (Hebrews 12:11).

Definition of discipline:

_____

_____

Purpose of discipline:

_____

_____

Reasons kids misbehave:

1. _____

2. _____

3. _____

What was Jesus' attitude toward children?

_____

_____

What kids need:

_____

_____

Three ways to communicate love:

1. _____

2. _____

3. _____

Three guidelines for safe touching:

1. _____

2. _____

3. _____

Training Session Two
Agreeing on a Discipline Plan for Your Church

1. Review Toss

You'll need a beanbag or a soft ball and a photocopy of the "Discipline Training: Session One Outline" handout (p. 148).

Say: **At our last meeting, we discussed some issues that are foundational to establishing a program of biblical discipline in our church. I'm going to toss this ball to someone. When the ball comes to you, stand up and tell one thing you learned in our last meeting.**

As you toss the ball, be prepared to prompt participants who are "stuck" for answers by giving clues from the "Discipline Training: Session One Outline."

Close the review by saying: **The first key to better behavior in the classroom is to see that kids' needs are met. Soon we'll begin to formulate our discipline guidelines for the whole church. But before we do that, let's look at two other keys to better behavior.**

2. Give Kids a Voice—Allow Choice

You'll need pencils, scissors, photocopies of the "Silly Instructions" handout (p. 153), and photocopies of the "Discipline Training: Session Two Outline" (p. 154).

Say: **To get a firsthand feeling of what it's like to be a child in a class, I'd like you to form groups of four.** Pause as participants do this and then say: **In your groups, decide who will be a One, a Two, a Three, and a Four.**

Give each group a pair of scissors and a set of instructions from the "Silly Instructions" handout (p. 153).

Say: **Cut your instructions into four sections, and give each person the appropriate section.**

Arbitrarily call on individuals to carry out their instructions in front of the whole group. For instance, you might say, "I'd like the One from this group to come up here with me and carry out his or her instructions." Call on different numbers from different groups until all four instructions have been carried out for each group. Then ask those who participated:

● **What was giving this "command performance" like for you?**

● **How is that like what happens to kids in our classes?**

Say: **Let's see what happens when I allow you to make choices.** Let everyone be seated in the large group again. Ask for two or three volunteers to carry out each instruction. Then ask:

● **How did allowing people to make choices change this experience?**

Distribute the "Discipline Training: Session Two Outline" handouts (p. 154) and pencils as you say: **Somehow having a choice makes all of the options look a little better. When kids are allowed to choose, they're more willing to invest themselves in an activity.** Ask:

● **What are some practical ways we can give kids choices in our classrooms?**

Say: **Even when we discipline children for acting out, we can offer choices. For instance, suppose Sherri refused to share materials in an art activity. You might say: "Sherri, the rule in our class is that we are kind to people. Sharing is one way to show kindness. Since you chose not to be kind in the art center, you may choose another center to work in, or you may sit in the time-out chair until the egg timer runs out. Then you may go back to the art center if you're prepared to be kind and share the materials.** Ask:

● **How will these choices help Sherri?**

Say: **The second key to better behavior is to allow kids to make choices. Now let's take a look at key number three.**

3. Say It, Show It, Live It

Say: **Children behave better when they see that we have high expectations for them and that we communicate and model those high expectations.**

Kids hate to disappoint their parents or teachers, so they intuitively look for the expectations of the adults around them. If they sense that a teacher does not expect them to behave well, they will act very much the way that the teacher expects. If, however, the teacher communicates high respect (both verbally and nonverbally), children are likely to live up to these high expectations. To state it simply, if you expect great things, you're likely to get them!

Ask:

● **What are some ways you could let your kids know your high expectations for them?**

● **What are some ways we might unwittingly let kids know that we expect them to misbehave?**

Say: **Expecting kids to behave well is just one third of the** keys to good behavior. The other two thirds are communicating and clarifying our expectations and modeling the behaviors we want kids to emulate. Ask:

● **As a teacher, what are some attitudes and behaviors you try to model for your kids each week?**

Say: **Let's look at how communicating and modeling high expectations plays out on different age levels. For instance, let's take the attitude of being kind.** Ask:

● **How would you model and communicate your expectation of kind behavior to preschoolers? to kindergartners? to early- and middle-elementary kids? to upper-elementary kids?**

Say: **One tool that helps communicate expectations to younger children is the "looks like, sounds like" question. You might ask: "What does being kind look like? What does it sound like?" You may want to ask that question every few weeks, just to remind children of your high expectations.**

4. Roll Out the Rules!

You'll need Bibles, a marker, and a dry-erase board or a large pad of newsprint. Option: You may want to photocopy and distribute the "Sample Discipline Policy" handouts on pages 155 and 156.

Say: **We've covered the basics of a biblical philosophy of discipline. Now it's time to put that philosophy to work as we formulate a unified discipline policy for our church. Now that we've laid the groundwork, formulating the rules will be easier than you think!**

Form small groups of teachers who work in each age level. Have them read the Scripture sources listed on the "Discipline Training: Session Two Outline" handouts and then formulate four to six rules or guidelines for behavior that they feel would work well in their classrooms. Allow about eight to ten minutes for brainstorming. Give a one-minute warning and then bring everyone together. Have a spokesperson from each group share that group's rules. Then, using a dry-erase board or large pad of newsprint, work as a whole group to synthesize no more than six basic rules that will work across the board in your church.

Have the teachers return to their age-level groups and brainstorm logical, age-appropriate consequences for breaking the rules and pleasant, positive consequences for obeying the rules. Again, allow eight to ten minutes for brainstorming. Give a one-minute warning and then bring everyone together. Have a spokesperson from each group share the consequences the members of his or her group have agreed on. Work together as a whole group to help each age-level group refine its lists of consequences.

If you have a fleet-fingered typist, you may want to type, photocopy, and distribute rule lists on the spot. Or have them available the following Sunday. Make sure rule lists are posted in each classroom.

Say: **Thanks for your hard work. Everyone in our church will benefit from the work we've done here. I have a poem I'd like to read to you to as a closing prayer. The language is a bit quaint and old-fashioned, but the message is timeless. The author is that famous character, A. Nonymous.**

> Dear Lord, I do not ask
> that thou shouldst give me some high work of thine—
> some noble calling
> or some wondrous task.
> Give me a little hand to hold in mine.
>
> Give me a little child to point the way
> over the strange, sweet path that leads to thee.
> Give me a little voice to pray; two shining eyes
> Thy face to see.
>
> The only crown I ask to wear, dear Lord, is this:
> That I may teach a little child.
> I do not ask that I may ever stand among the wise or
> worthy or the great.
> I only ask that softly, hand in hand, a child and I may enter
> at the gate.
> Amen.

Silly Instructions

One: Sing "Happy Birthday to You" in an operatic voice.

Two: Say "She sells seashells down by the seashore" five times fast.

Three: Do your best imitation of John Wayne.

Four: Open your mouth wide, and try to wiggle your ears.

One: Sing "Happy Birthday to You" in an operatic voice.

Two: Say "She sells seashells down by the seashore" five times fast.

Three: Do your best imitation of John Wayne.

Four: Open your mouth wide, and try to wiggle your ears.

Discipline Training: Session Two Outline

Keys to better behavior:

1. _____

2. _____

3. _____

Basic rule brainstorms
Scripture sources: Matthew 7:12; Matthew 22:37-40; Philippians 2:1b-2.

Rule 1:_____

Rule 2:_____

Rule 3:_____

Rule 4:_____

Rule 5:_____

Rule 6:_____

Positive consequences for following the rules:

_____

_____

_____

Negative consequences for disobeying the rules:

_____

_____

_____

Sample Discipline Policy

(You may want to use this handout as a starting point for creating your own discipline policy.)

Elementary Department

Rules We Obey to Show Our Love for God and God's People

1. Respect other people.
2. One person speaks at a time.
3. Obey directions the first time.
4. There will be no bathroom or drink breaks during class.
5. Wear name tags appropriately.
6. Respect church property.

Positive Consequences

 1. Learn about and please God.

 3. Get a "Hooray!" letter sent home.

 2. Know you've done a good job!

 4. Surprise celebrations.

Negative Consequences

 1. Receive a verbal warning.

 4. Contact parents.

2. Attend a teacher-student conference.

5. Sign a contract for appropriate behavior made with teacher, parent, and student.

3. Time-out away from group.

(For negative consequences 4 and 5, a children's ministry leader should be involved.)

Sample Discipline Policy

(You may want to use this handout as a starting
point for creating your own discipline policy.)

Preschool Department
Rules We Obey to Show Our Love for God and God's People

 1. Use kind words.

 2. Listen when someone
else is talking.

 3. Obey directions the
first time.

 4. Raise your hand if you
want to talk.

 5. Use an indoor voice.

Positive Consequences

 1. Learn about and
please God.

 3. Get a "Hooray!" letter
sent home.

 2. Know you've done a
good job!

 4. Surprise celebrations.

Negative Consequences

 1. Receive a verbal warning.

 4. Contact parents.

 2. Attend a teacher-stu-
dent conference.

5. Sign a contract for
appropriate behavior
made with teacher,
parent, and student.

 3. Time-out away from
group.

*(For negative consequences 4 and 5, a chil-
dren's ministry leader should be involved.)*

About the Authors

Jody Capehart has been in education for over twenty-five years. She founded a Christian school and served as its principal for fifteen years. She served as the director of children's ministries at Grace Bible Church in Dallas, Texas for eight years, and she has helped start several other schools. She is currently the principal of Prestonwood Christian Academy, a new learning-style-based school in Dallas. A popular speaker at conventions and workshops nationwide, Jody has authored ten books including *Cherishing and Challenging Your Children, Becoming a Treasured Teacher, Once Upon a Time,* and *You and Your ADD Child.* Jody is married to Paul Capehart, who plays horn in the Dallas Symphony Orchestra. They have three children, ages twenty-three, sixteen, and twelve.

Gordon and Becki West are founders and codirectors of "Kids at Heart," a Christian education consulting ministry based in Mesa, Arizona. They work both individually and as a team in writing, consulting, and speaking to parents and educators who work with children from birth through high school age. Gordon is currently the children's pastor at Central Christian Church in Mesa, Arizona. He was a contributor to Michael Lawson and Robert Choun's book, *Directing Christian Education.* Becki is an active volunteer in LiveWires Ministries for fifth and sixth graders at Central Christian Church. Previously she was the associate for young families at an independent church in Tucson, Arizona, where she conducted research and training in equipping parents and teachers. She has taught in the public schools of Los Angeles, Denver, Colorado Springs, and Tucson. Gordon and Becki are popular workshop speakers and have authored several articles for Children's Ministry Magazine. They currently serve as church consultants for Group Publishing. The Wests have two girls, ages four and eight.

Bibliography

Annotated Bibliography for Parents and Teachers
The Discipline Guide for Children's Ministry
Jody Capehart, Becki West, and Gordon West

- Ames, Dr. Louis Bates. *He Hit Me First.* New York, NY: Dember Books, 1982.
  This book from child development expert Dr. Louis Bates Ames takes a look at children and explains the discipline issue from the developmental perspective.

- Armstrong, Thomas. *In Their Own Way.* New York, NY: St. Martin's Press, 1987.
  Dr. Thomas Armstrong is a learning disabilities specialist who takes the writings of Dr. Howard Gardner and puts them into a very "reader-friendly" form to help explain that children learn in their own way.

- Armstrong, Thomas. *7 Kinds of Smart.* New York, NY: Penguin Books, 1993.
  Dr. Thomas Armstrong delineates the different levels of intelligence, presents ways to identify each level, and shows how to teach to children's intelligence strengths so that each can be smart!

- Armstrong, Thomas. *Multiple Intelligences in the Classroom.* Alexandria, VA: Association for Supervision and Curriculum Development, 1994.
  This book is a must for teachers, home-schoolers, and parents committed to helping their children learn each subject through their own intelligence strengths.

- Butler, Kathleen. *It's All in Your Mind: A Student's Guide to Learning Style.* Columbia, CT: The Learners Dimension, 1988.
  Dr. Butler has written a workbook to be used with teenagers to help them identify their learning styles in order to be better students.

- Butler, Kathleen. *A Teacher's Guide to It's All in Your Mind.* Columbia, CT: The Learners Dimension, 1988.
  Dr. Butler has developed each lesson plan stylistically so that teachers can teach students about style using style! This book provides excellent bridging techniques as well.

- Capehart, Jody. *Cherishing and Challenging Your Children.* Wheaton, IL: Victor Books, 1991.
  This book is a practical guide to help parents to better understand how personalities, modalities, and learning styles impact the home scene. Each of these concepts is applied to such topics as desirable discipline, communication, enriching the environment, self-esteem, spiritual development, and more. To order, call 972-239-3850.

- Capehart, Jody. *Becoming a Treasured Teacher.* Wheaton, IL: Victor Books, 1992.
  This book synthesizes various learning models and provides a simpler model to apply to the practical aspects of the teaching process. It covers topics such as lesson planning, teaching with centers, discipline, and more.

- Capehart, Jody, and Paul Warren. *You and Your ADD Child.* Nashville, TN: Thomas Nelson Publishers, 1995.
  This book is a very comprehensive guide to understanding Attention Deficit Disorder in children. It provides medical background as well as practical helps for the home, school, and church.

- Christie, Les. *How To Work With Rude, Obnoxious and Apathetic Kids*. Wheaton, IL: Victor Books, 1994.

  This book looks at many of the issues that drive adults "up the wall" in dealing with today's kids, including kids with A.D.D., and provides practical helps to dealing with these tough issues.

- Dobson, James. *Dare to Discipline*. Wheaton, IL: Tyndale House Publishers, 1991.

  This book is the "bible" for discipline with children. Dr. Dobson shares his great wisdom through practical insights into methods of disciplining children based upon godly principles.

- Dobson, James. *The Strong-Willed Child*. Wheaton, IL: Tyndale House Publishers, 1985.

  This book is a "must" for any parent or teacher dealing with a strong-willed child. This child can be brought to discipline, and Dr. Dobson shows us how to best accomplish this most important task.

- Dunn, Dr. Rita, Dr. Kenneth Dunn, and Dr. Donald Treffinger. *Bringing Out the Giftedness in Your Child*. New York, NY: John Wiley and Sons, Inc., 1992.

  This book shows ways to nurture every child's unique strengths, talents, and potential.

- Fuller, Cheri. *Home Life*. Tulsa, OK: Honor Books, 1988.

  This book helps parents to understand how their children learn, how to help them be all they can be, and how to work with the school and facilitate the homework scene.

- Gardner, Howard. *Frames of Mind: The Theory of Multiple Intelligence*. New York, NY: Basic Books, 1983.

  Dr. Gardner develops a model of seven intelligences that shows how each individual learns differently. He also shows that if people are taught through their intelligence strengths, they could learn at a higher rate.

- Gardner, Howard. *The Unschooled Mind: How Children Think and How Schools Should Teach*. New York, NY: Basic Books, 1983.

  Dr. Gardner merges cognitive science with an educational agenda to show how ill-suited people's minds and natural patterns of learning are to current educational materials, practices, and institutions. He also makes an eloquent case for restructuring our schools.

- Golstein, Sam. *Why Won't My Child Pay Attention?* (video). Salt Lake City, UT: Neurology, Learning, and Behavior Center, 1990.

  This is an excellent video to help parents better understand what Attention Deficit Disorder is and how to deal with it in practical ways.

- Gregorc, Anthony. *An Adult's Guide to Style*. Columbia, CT: Gregorc Associates, Inc., 1982.

  This book explains the Gregorc model for learning styles. This book is for the serious student of learning styles. Dr. Gregorc also created a Gregorc Style Delineator available for students who want to discover their learning styles. This tool is available through Gregorc Associates, Inc., 15 Doubleday Road, P.O. Box 351, Columbia, CT 06237-0351.

- Haazen, Barbara Shook. *Even If I Did Something Awful*. New York, NY: Aladdin, 1992.

  This is a delightful children's book that reflects a child's desire to know if a parent would still love him even if he did something really, truly awful.

- Kohlenberger, Carolyn, and Noel Wescombe. *Raising Wise Children—How to Teach Your Child to Think*. Portland, OR: Multnomah Press, 1990.

  This book provides practical ways to help children learn to make wise decisions and think through issues.

- Kroeger, Otto, and Janet M. Theusen. *Type Talk*. New York, NY: Delacorte Press, 1988.

  This easy-to-read book about the Myers-Briggs version of Carl Jung's personality types is loaded with anecdotal stories to better explain this more detailed personality model.

- LaHaye, Dr. Tim. *Transformed Temperaments*. Wheaton, IL: Tyndale House Publishers, 1971.
  This book clearly defines each of the temperaments and combinations based upon the Hippocrates model.

- Littauer, Florence. *Raising the Curtain on Raising Children*. Dallas, TX: Word Publishing, 1988.
  This book helps us to understand temperament tendencies in children based upon the Hippocrates model.

- Martin, Grant. *The Hyperactive Child*. Wheaton, IL: Victor Books, 1992.
  This book provides information on the identification of A.D.H.D. and sources of treatment.

- McDowell, Josh and Bob Hostetler. *Right From Wrong*. Dallas, TX: Word Publishing, 1994.
  This book is a must for teachers and parents to help them better understand the culture that we are living in today and why it is hard for our young people to be disciplined and to determine right from wrong. This book provides the practical tools necessary to reverse this trend.

- Neff, LaVonne. *One of a Kind*. Portland, OR: Multnomah Press, 1988.
  This book uses the Myers-Briggs personality profile to help us better understand our children.

- *Personal Profile System*. Minneapolis, MN: Carlson Learning Company, 1994.
  For more information about the *Personal Profile System*® and DiSC®, or other Carlson Learning Company learning resources, call 800-777-9897, or write to Carlson Learning Company, P.O. Box 59159, Minneapolis, Minnesota, 55459-8247.

- Rohm, Dr. Robert. *Positive Personality Insights*. Columbus, GA: Brentwood Christian Press, 1992.
  This book provides helpful and humorous ways to better understand and apply the DISC model.

- Swindoll, Charles R. *You and Your Child: A Biblical Guide for Nurturing Confident Children From Infancy to Independence*. Colorado Springs, CO: Focus on the Family, 1994.
  An eye-opening book for parents who want to instill lasting moral and spiritual values in their children. Using Scripture, Dr. Swindoll presents the value in each child's individuality.

- Tobias, Cynthia. *The Way They Learn: How to Discover and Teach to Your Child's Strengths*. Colorado Springs, CO: Focus on the Family, 1994.
  This book takes a look at various learning models in order to help parents and teachers better understand how children learn.

- Voges, Ken and Dr. Ron Braund. *Understanding Why Others Misunderstand You*. Chicago, IL: Moody Press, Inc., 1994.
  This book provides very helpful ways to understand your personality type on the DISC model and how you interact with each of the other personalities.

- Wlodkowski, Raymond, and Judith Jaynes. *Eager to Learn: Helping Children Become Motivated and Love Learning*. San Francisco, CA: Jossey Bass Publishers, 1990.
  This book provides a wealth of ways to help students become more motivated in the learning process thus fostering success in learning.